ST. PETER CANISIUS.

(From the contemporary painting in the possession of the Diocesan Seminary Fribourg, Switzerland. Artist unknown.)

A CHAMPION OF
THE CHURCH
ST. PETER CANISIUS, S.J.

BY THE

REV. WILLIAM REANY, D.D.

Author of " The Creation of the Human Soul," etc.

New York, Cincinnati, Chicago, San Francisco

BENZIGER BROTHERS

PRINTERS TO THE HOLY APOSTOLIC SEE

1931

PROTESTATION

The Author desires it to be understood that, unless where he expressly states that the Church or the Holy See has recognised the truth of miracles or other supernatural manifestations referred to in the following pages, he claims no credence for them beyond what the available historical evidence may warrant.

𝔑ihil 𝔒bstat:

JOANNES KELLY,
Censor Theol. Depu.

𝔍mprimi potest:

✠ EDUARDUS,
Archiep. Dublinen.,
Hiberniae Primas.

DUBLINI, *die 2° Septembris, anno* 1931.

First published November 1931

CONTENTS

INTRODUCTION

THE invention of printing in the middle of the fifteenth century by John Gutenberg[1] should be classed with the greatest events in the history of the world. It caused a revolution in the development of culture, equalled by hardly any other incident in the Christian era. Facility in disseminating the treasures of the intellect was a necessary condition for the rapid development of the sciences in modern times.

Happening, as it did, just at the time when science was becoming more secularised and its cultivation no longer left almost entirely to the monks, it may be said that the age

[1] " Printing from fixed type, which is really a species of engraving, seems to have been used to a limited extent in very ancient times. The invention of printing from movable metal types is claimed for two printers—Laurence Coster of Haarlem and John Gutenberg of Mainz. The latter set up a printing press at Mainz about 1450. Printing was practically confined to Mainz till the sack of the town, in 1462, dispersed the printers, and led to the more general adoption of the art. William Caxton, the first English printer, learnt the secret while resident in the Low Countries, and set up a printing press at Westminster in 1476."—*Pannell's Reference Book*, p. 330.

was pregnant with the invention. Thus not only is Gutenberg's art inseparable from the growth of modern times, but it has been an indispensable factor in the education of the people at large. Culture and knowledge, until then considered aristocratic privileges peculiar to certain classes, were popularised by typography, although in the process it unfortunately brought about an internal revolution in the intellectual world in the direction of what is profane and free from restraint.

The invention of printing, besides exerting a great influence on literature in general and on education in particular, gave birth to a new species of literature, namely, publications appearing at intervals, either regular or irregular. These sheets or broadsides, as they were called, dealing mostly with religious and political events, can be traced back to the year 1493. The oldest existing broadsides were published in Germany. The earliest Italian periodicals were the *Notizie Scritte* of Florence, which were called Gazetta, from the coin paid for reading them. This is the origin of the title *Gazette* given to some English newspapers. These early precursors of the modern newspapers were, of course, very rudimentary, and without any set form or scheme. From the first, however, religious interest found an echo in them. The broadsides were later succeeded by the *Relations* and the title of the Jesuit *Relations*, which has become almost a household word in American history, shows how early the Church authorities appreciated the possibilities of this new kind of publication.

No Catholic work in these days is more important than the work of the Catholic Press. This has been the verdict of Rome and of the Episcopate. They have urged the obligation upon us in stronger language than any Catholic journalist would have dared to use. They have declared their conviction that the defence of Catholic interests is so closely bound up in these days with the Press which forms men's minds, that all other social and charitable work will certainly be hampered unless the Catholic Press is supported. The welfare of the Catholic Church in any country depends very much upon the condition of the Catholic Press. Wherever the apostolate of the Catholic Press is zealously and methodically taken up, Catholic life revives, Catholic institutions flourish, Catholic principles are held in honour, and Catholic rights are defended.

Pope Leo XIII wrote an Encyclical on August 1st, 1897, to the Bishops of Germany, Austria, and Switzerland, on the occasion of the tercentenary of the death of St. Peter Canisius, in which he says :—

"There is a certain resemblance between our times and the period in which Canisius lived, an epoch in which the desire for innovation and freedom in religious thought were followed by a decrease in Faith and very great laxity in morals. The deliverance from this two-fold pest of all classes of society, and especially youth, was the end in view of him who, after Boniface, was the Apostle of Germany. The means which he employed for this purpose were not only public speaking and conferences, but also, particularly, the foundation of schools and the writing of excellent books.

" In accordance with his example many among you have employed these same means with enthusiasm against very cunning enemies, and have not ceased, in the defence and honour of religion, to study the highest sciences and to cultivate the liberal arts. In this they have been supported by the explicit approval of the Roman Pontiffs, whose constant preoccupation has always been to maintain the ancient lustre of learning and to help the progress of civilization in all its branches. You are not ignorant, Venerable Brethren, that we ourselves have always at heart to attend chiefly to the good education of youth, and that we have secured it everywhere as far as it has been in our power.

" Willingly do we avail ourselves of this opportunity to bring forward the valiant leader, Peter Canisius, as a model to all who fight for Christ in the Army of the Church, so that they may be convinced that the weapons of science must be joined to the justice of the cause, and in order to be thus enabled to defend religion in a more vigorous and efficient manner."

The latest bibliography of the Society of Jesus devotes thirty-eight quarto pages to a list of the works published by St. Peter Canisius, and their different editions; and it must be added that this list is incomplete. In an Address delivered on March 20th, 1925, Pope Pius XI said that St. Peter Canisius "has become one of the Creators of the Catholic Press and especially of the Catholic periodical." The following pages give a brief outline of the life of this truly remarkable man, who was canonized and declared a Doctor of the Church on the Feast of the Ascension, May 21st, 1925.

W. R.

FEAST OF THE ASSUMPTION OF OUR LADY,
    August 15th, 1931.

CHAPTER I

HIS TIMES AND OURS

THE sixteenth century, the period in which St. Peter Canisius, Doctor of the Universal Church, lived and laboured, had these characteristics in common with the early decades of the twentieth century, namely, that it was a time of religious, political and social unrest. Germany and Switzerland, the two countries which were to witness most of his activities, were the battle-ground of the Reformers, who opposed to the doctrines of the supremacy of St. Peter and the Sacrifice of the Mass, first the principle of the immediate guidance of the Soul by the Holy Ghost, or private judgment, which radically subverted all Church Authority, and notably that of the Supreme Pontiff; and, secondly, the principle of justification by Faith alone, which practically subverted the whole Sacramental and Sacrificial System, with the priestly ministry that it postulates.

The first impulse to secession from the Catholic Church in Germany had been supplied by the opposition of Luther to the Proclamation of Indulgences by Pope Leo X for those who contributed to the completion of St. Peter's Basilica in Rome. In assailing the abuses of Indulgences in general, Luther voiced a wide-spread feeling in Germany, and gained adherents among men of influence in Church and State.

In the German-speaking parts of Switzerland Zwingli inaugurated the so-called Reformation, which spread there with great rapidity. Interesting to relate, the Canton of Fribourg, the principal scene of the labours of the last years of St. Peter Canisius, escaped the contagion. Zwingli was followed by Calvin, who directed the recently founded University of Geneva, the Mecca of Protestantism. The so-called Reformers, who acquired the name of Protestants by solemnly protesting against the propositions of the Diet of Spires in 1529, were confronted by the true Reformers of Holy Church, not the least of whom was Peter Canisius, who was chosen by God in those days to raise up the Tabernacle of David that was fallen, and to close up the breaches of the walls thereof, and to repair what was fallen and to rebuild it as in days of old (cf. Amos ix. 2).

St. Bede the Venerable, Father of English History, in his Preface to *The Ecclesiastical History of the English Nation*, thus commends the study of the sayings and actions of former men of renown : " For if history relates good things of good men, the attentive hearer is excited to imitate that which is good ; or if it mentions evil things of wicked persons, nevertheless the religious and pious hearer or reader, shunning that which is hurtful and perverse, is more earnestly excited to perform those things which he knows to be good and worthy of God."

St. Peter Canisius, although not one of the first companions of St. Ignatius Loyola, was nevertheless one of the earliest members of the Society of Jesus, being received into it by Blessed Peter Faber. The object of the following narrative is to make more widely known to the English-speaking world the life-story of one too little known to the present generation, but which is not without its interest and lessons for those living to-day.

Raised to the honour of the Altar by Holy Church, St. Peter Canisius combined in his life the farsightedness of a prophet and the energy of a man of action to a remarkable degree. Intensely human, it may be said of him that " he loved justice and hated iniquity " (cf. Ps. xliv. 8).

The weapons he used were the weapons of argument, of persuasion and charity. The sword which he drew against the Children of Unbelief was " the sword of the Spirit, which is the Word of God " (cf. Heb. iv. 12). The fire which he lighted against them was the fire of Divine Love, which the Saviour of Mankind came to enkindle in the hearts of men.

At the present day it is said that the people of England are lapsing back into Paganism. Be this as it may, it is well to remember that it is not by coercion, but by the willing surrender of the citadel of the heart, that men and women are converted ; and that in passing from Pagan to Christian civilisation we have passed from darkness to light, from Egyptian bondage to the liberty of the Children of God. " For you are bought with a great price " (1 Cor. vi. 20). In his day, as in our own, the evil that boded mischief to Germany and Switzerland, and which bodes mischief to our own country, arose and arises from the defective system of school education. He understood that to educate means to bring out, to develop the intellectual, moral and religious faculties of the soul. An education that improves the mind and memory to the neglect of religious and moral training is but an imperfect system.

He was aware that, however eminently useful the development of the intellect of a youth may be, it is more important that he should be familiar with and master of the great problems of life, his origin, destiny, and the means of attaining it. He endeavoured to make the children who came under his sway not only learned but pious, not merely polished members of society but conscientious Christians, giving them a training which formed their hearts as well as their minds; in a word, making them not only men of the world but also men of God.

He saw that the divorce of religious from secular education inflicted a wound on the soul which frequently fomented the spirit of indifference in matters of faith, and tended to paralyse the will in matters of morals. So, too, in our days the moral and intellectual growth of our children must go hand in hand. Otherwise what is intended to be a blessing may prove to be a curse. The ship that is destined to sail on a rough and perilous voyage should be well ballasted. The only sure way to preserve the blessings of Christian civilisation is to inculcate in the minds of youth the virtues of justice, honesty and truth, together with those other fundamental duties which are taught by the Founder of Christianity.

> There is a tide in the affairs of men,
> Which taken at the flood leads on to fortune.

CHAPTER II

EARLY YEARS OF ST. PETER CANISIUS

NYMWEGEN, where St. Peter Canisius was born, is a part of Gueldre, a Province of Holland.[1] It is situated on the left bank of the Waal, the larger and more beautiful of the two arms formed by the River Rhine on its entry into the Netherlands. This town existed at the period when the Romans were masters of the country. Charlemagne selected it as one of his chief residences and built a castle there with a chapel, which recalls the plan of the Cathedral of Aix-la-Chapelle. The old sanctuary is still standing ; but the castle, which several emperors, particularly Frederick Barbarossa, had greatly enlarged, was destroyed during the Revolution in 1795.

Among the remains are to be seen the apse of a second chapel, dating from the time of Barbarossa. This locality, with its old ruins, its large trees and its beautiful view over

[1] Although Nymwegen is to-day a flourishing Dutch town, yet at the time of the birth of St. Peter Canisius it possessed the privileges of a German Reichstadt, and belonged ecclesiastically to the Archdiocese of Cologne.

the river, is, to-day, still one of the most attractive walks in the town. In the Middle Ages Nymwegen was very prosperous. Since 1248 it belonged to the Counts of Gueldre, who later became Dukes of Gueldre. The beautiful Church of St. Stephen dates from the thirteenth century, in which St. Peter Canisius prayed in his childhood. Not far from this church, which is now Protestant, is a Latin or Ecclesiastical school, where he commenced his studies.

St. Peter Canisius was born in a house of the Broerstraat (Rue des Frères), a house which has long since been demolished. In 1591 the town fell into the hands of the Calvinists. Churches and convents were confiscated and the Catholic religion forbidden under the most severe penalties. In spite of persecution most of the Catholics remained undaunted. They were encouraged by Dominicans, Minorites and Jesuits who, banished from the town, returned secretly to celebrate Mass and administer the Sacraments. This situation lasted with little improvement until the Revolution, which, in 1795, proclaimed equality of religious worship. When Louis Buonaparte, brother of Napoleon I, became King of Holland, he restored to the Catholics some of their churches. Just before our own time, Nymwegen has been wonderfully developed. It is now a beautiful modern town of seventy thousand inhabitants, two-thirds of whom are Catholics. They possess a dozen churches and numerous schools, amongst others a college named after St. Peter Canisius, which is directed by the Jesuits and is well attended. The Catholics of Holland, who are well organised and exercise a great influence in the affairs of their country, founded in 1923, in the native town of St. Peter Canisius, a University, which is protected by the famous Dutchman whom Pius XI has proclaimed a Saint and a Doctor of the Church.

Among the families who in times of persecution were distinguished for their loyalty to the Catholic faith, that of Canisius must be reckoned. This family bears different names in documents, but the sense is the same, and is recalled by the coats-of-arms, which invariably give a representation of a dog, the symbol of vigilance and fidelity. Thus it is to be found on the most ancient of nine seals of James Kanis, the father of Peter Canisius, which are preserved in the Town Hall of Nymwegen.

James Kanis, whose ancestors were established in this town in the middle of the fifteenth century, studied law in different places, especially in the University of Paris. He became tutor of the children of René II, Duke of Lorraine, the ally of the Swiss in the wars against Burgundy. James Kanis, who enjoyed a great reputation at the Court of Lorraine and was ennobled in return for his services, after some years returned to his country. The inhabitants of Nymwegen were not slow in showing the greatest respect to their compatriot, who was a distinguished lawyer, clever administrator and a good Catholic, " strongly attached to the Catholic religion," as his son Peter testifies. He was nine times Burgomaster. On several occasions he was appointed to represent the interests of his town and to defend them against neighbouring sovereigns.

James Kanis was married twice. His first wife, Aegidia van Houweningen, had two children, Peter and Wendeline, who were still young when she died. She was remarkable for her lively faith and solid piety. Her son recalls a noteworthy instance. " Before dying," he relates, " she called her husband, put him on his guard against the new doctrines, and recommended him always to remain loyal to the faith of his ancestors." The second wife of James Kanis was Wendeline van Bergh, a sister of Canon Boucard, who sought, in 1553, to have Peter Canisius nominated to the See of Vienna. The holy religious, as is well known, did not accept the Episcopate, not out of fear of work, but out of humility and to obey the Constitutions of his Order. In order to show that he was not seeking the worldly promotion of his family and how distasteful to him was the intervention of the good Canon, he remarked, " If I am made Bishop, people will say it was my uncle, and not the Holy Spirit, who selected me."

By his second marriage James Kanis had several children, eight according to most historians. When in 1565 Peter Canisius, at that time Provincial of his Order and Delegate of the Pope, visited his native town—which he was never to see again— he met there his sister Wendeline, wife of Godefroid van Triest, who was Burgomaster of Nymwegen, also his brother Theodoric, a Jesuit and Rector of the College of Dillingen, and his sister Clare, who had become a Poor Clare, and who was later Abbess of the

Convent of Wamel. In addition three sisters
and a brother of Peter Canisius, all of whom
were married in Nymwegen, came to greet
him and to present their children. Moreover,
he had two other brothers who dwelt in a
neighbouring town. It is thus evident that
the posterity of James Kanis was numerous.
All his sons and daughters paid him the
greatest honour. Father Hasius, a contemporary, declares that in 1613 the one hundred
and fifty descendants of this respectable
family all practised faithfully the religion of
their ancestors. Vocations to the priesthood
and to the religious life were numerous in
this family. Before the end of the seventeenth century, one reckoned fifteen. In our
days a certain number of Catholic families
in Holland can claim the honour of descent
from that of Canisius, from which has issued
one of the best servants of the Church and
one of the greatest saints of the sixteenth
century.

The *Confessions* of Peter Canisius and his
Testament are two works in which he gives
many details of his life, particularly concerning his infancy and boyhood. When
reading these writings one must bear in mind
that it is a saint who speaks. He considers

his actions in the light of a lively faith and
with much humility, severely reproaching
himself for his faults and slightest defects,
while almost always passing over in silence
his acts of virtue. Thus, in his *Confessions*,
which he wrote in Latin at Dillingen about
1570, we read these words :—" O Eternal
Wisdom ! Thou hast deigned to enlighten
me in order that my soul should know itself
and be humbled by the truth. . . . By the
brightness of Thy light I understand, O my
God, that the knowledge of myself princi-
pally consists in seeing clearly that of my
nature I am nothing at all, I am worth
nothing, I can do nothing and I have nothing
at all ; for from Thee alone depends the
beginning, the middle, and the end of every
good work." Likewise, in his *Testament*,
which he dictated in Latin a little time before
his death in 1596 or 1597, and which he
calls, " The Summary of the Benefits which
God has heaped upon me," the holy old man
said : " It is just that God, the beginning
and end of all things, should be glorified, not
only in great but also in the least things. For
this reason no one will blame me, I hope, if
I manifest by this writing the continual
mixture of good and evil which is found in

3

me, a mean creature, in order that God may thereby be known and praised." It was in the pursuit of the greatest glory of God that Peter Canisius found his inspiration in the pages in which he speaks of himself. These works contain excellent lessons of piety, work, and prudence, especially for children and young people. They also demonstrate that he who wrote them knew how to remain perfectly humble all through life.

He speaks of his birth in the following manner: "In the year 1521 after Thy Nativity, O Christ Jesus! I was born. My father was called James and my mother Aegidia; both were Catholics and both descended from rich and honourable families. These are the benefits of Thy love; equally by disposition of Thy providence, the town of Nymwegen in the country of Gueldre was my fatherland; also by a particular gift of Thy grace the same day, namely, the 8th May, the Feast of the Apparition of St. Michael the Archangel, was my birthday, and many years after my baptism was the date of my religious profession." Our Saint carefully relates the two events of his life connected with the Feast of St. Michael, namely, his birth and his admission into the

Society of Jesus ; for he appears to have had a special devotion to the Archangel. If his *Confessions* had been written at the end of his life, he could have added that it was in the College of Fribourg, placed by him under the patronage of St. Michael, that he passed the last seventeen years of his life. To-day, in the room where he died, and which, in the seventeenth century, was converted into a chapel, may be seen a picture of the Archangel, which was formerly in the private chapel of Peter Canisius, and before which he often said Mass. Lastly, it is in the Church of St. Michael that his relics are to be found, where they have rested since 1625.

There is another coincidence which historians narrate in connection with the birth of Peter Canisius. On the 8th May, 1521, the Decree of the Emperor Charles V was issued, by which Luther was placed under the ban of the Empire for refusing to retract his errors. At the end of this same month of May, in the same year, 1521, a young Spanish captain, Ignatius of Loyola, was wounded in the defence of the town of Pampeluna. This event led him to change his life and thus remotely prepared the foundation of the

Society of Jesus, of which Canisius was later
to become one of the most illustrious members.

St. Peter Canisius did not enjoy the care
of his mother for long. He was still young
when she died, after receiving a promise
from her husband to remain faithful to the
Catholic religion. The holy Jesuit never
forgot his mother, whom he had scarcely
known. He knew that she had often recommended him to God with fervour and
tears. Forty years later he prayed to God
in the following terms : " O Eternal God,
I pray Thee, by Thy infinite charity, to
remit all the stains in my father and mother
which Thy justice still finds in them. This
is the request which their son makes to Thee
on his knees by the Precious Blood of Thy
Christ."

James Kanis, with two young children,
Peter and a younger sister, Wendeline, married
again. His second wife, Wendeline van
Bergh, a native of Nymwegen and a fervent
Catholic, was a true mother to the children
of Aegidia. She was seconded in her solicitude by a pious person, perhaps her sister,
who often came to visit her and exercised
a welcome influence over Peter. " At this
period of my life," he says, " by a secret

movement, which I attribute to my angel guardian, I began to find pleasure in seeing holy pictures and the ceremonies of the Church. Willingly I served the priest at the altar, and I, myself, although I was quite a child, loved to practise the duties of a priest, to imitate what he did, singing, offering the sacrifice of the Mass and saying prayers, in one word, to reproduce as far as I could, in the presence of my companions, the ceremonies of the Mass. These are, if one so wishes, the innocent games of children; but these games sometimes manifest signs of character. . . . Now children are treated differently and wrongly. People take away from them what can nourish their simple piety."

James Kanis saw his family increase ; but he was fully occupied as Burgomaster, and could not, it seems, take sufficient care of his eldest son Peter, who was intelligent, lively, and readily joined in the games of his companions. " Alas," he exclaims in his *Confessions*, " how many hours and days have I lost in trifles. I occupied most of my time in doing nothing, playing, amusing myself, running here and there, quite engrossed in the thousand trifles which so seriously occupy childhood. These empty pleasures pursued me even into church and during my prayers. How many times have I failed my parents, my companions, and all those who addressed any warning to me!" Besides these weaknesses one may clearly discern in Peter Canisius sincere piety, and at an early age a desire to know the designs of God in his regard. " I was a child growing up," he relates, " when one day I was praying in the Church of St. Stephen at Nymwegen and adoring on my knees Thy Sacred Body, I received from Thy bounty, O Saviour, a grace which I cannot forget. I called upon Thee with anxiety, seeing through the vanities of the world, its foolish errors, and the thousand dangers which threatened my life and my salvation. I entreated Thee in words like these : ' O Lord ! make me know Thy ways and teach me Thy path.' " In truth, this grace, so much desired, the fear of the Divine Judgment, was granted to him, " as a saving bridle, which prevented him from running in the ways of evil."

CHAPTER III

STUDIES AND ADMISSION INTO THE SOCIETY OF JESUS

At the age of eleven or twelve years Peter Canisius was sent to begin his literary studies at the Apostolic Latin School of Nymwegen. These new surroundings were not without danger for him. " I found," he said, " companions whose words and example taught me evil and encouraged me to commit it. O Lord, I do not accuse them in order to excuse myself. They sinned and I had my share in their sin. They deserved the rod, and I, like them, deserved it also."

God, however, did not allow the young student to be overcome amid these dangers which threatened his purity of soul. The Papal Brief of the Beatification of Peter Canisius, issued by Pope Pius IX on August 2nd, 1865, says that he " kept his robe of innocence until his last breath." He himself, in his *Confessions*, clearly manifests that with the help of God he had repelled serious temptations : " Oh, if young people who are

still innocent knew their happiness, with
what love and vigilance they would protect
this inestimable treasure against all dangers.
What struggles they would make to defend
it ! What zeal they would show in watching
and conquering the enemy who fights against
them ! Surely I have no right to glory in
the chastity of my soul and body. I know
well that of myself I cannot protect my
purity. It is Thy gift, O Saviour ! it is Thou
alone by Thy grace Who not only makes
possible the yoke of chastity but renders it
easy, agreeable, and sweet."

Not only at Nymwegen, but especially at
Cologne, was Peter Canisius victorious in the
combat. In the beginning of the year 1536
he went to Cologne to continue his studies,
and he writes in his *Confessions* as follows :
" O God, Thou hast inspired in my father
the idea of sending me to Cologne to pursue
higher and better studies under good masters.
. . . Thou has given me generous hospitality
in the house of Andrew Bardwick, a venerable
theologian. Thou hast given me in the place
of a father, Nicholas van Esch, a priest of
uncommon piety. In those first years Thou
hast obtained for me a dwelling spacious as
well as religious in the (hostel) Martyrs d'Or,

or, as the name is to-day, St. Géréon. The town besides provided for me in the College Du Mont every facility for my instruction and education. It is there that I finished my literary education and received the degree of Master of Arts. Such was Thy will." The College Du Mont was part of the University. Peter Canisius finished his literary studies in a brilliant manner, as may be seen from the facility in which he expressed himself in different languages later, especially in Latin. On the 2nd November, 1536, he became a Bachelor of Arts. On the 15th March, 1538, he obtained the Licentiate, and on the 25th May, 1540, when he was nineteen years old, he received the degree of Master of Arts, that is to say, the Doctorate of Philosophy. These successes required constant work, which left little time for pleasure.

The enthusiasm of the young student was thus safeguarded by his Christian sentiments and great piety. He had the good fortune of meeting in Cologne two men who were well qualified to advise and direct him ; the first was Andrew Bardwick, the master of a hostel, a Canon of St. Géréon, a church dedicated to some soldiers of the Theban

legion, who were martyred at Cologne.
This church, by reason of its numerous
gilded objects is called the *Martyrs d'Or*
(Golden Martyrs). Hence the name of the
house which Canon Bardwick occupied at
that time. In the same hostel lived the
second, a very pious young priest named
Nicholas van Esch. Canisius chose him for
his spiritual director. Nicholas van Esch was
very friendly with the Carthusian monks of
Cologne, who held him in great esteem and
reserved a cell for him, where he often made
spiritual exercises. Thus it was that Peter
Canisius came into contact with the Car-
thusians, whose example had a great influence
on his vocation.

A fact is recorded by Father Hasius, a
contemporary, which gives a glimpse into
the room occupied by Peter Canisius as a
student. He refers to a man of Cologne
who, about the year 1573, speaks as follows : [1]
" My father had in our town a studio for
bookbinding when Peter Canisius attended
the lectures of the University. From time
to time I was sent to deliver to the young
student some books which we had bound for
him. I went there trembling, because on

[1] *Saint Pierre Canisius*, by E. Morand ; Fribourg, 1925, p. 18.

the table there was a skull." Peter Canisius, in spite of his austerities, won the affections of his fellow-students and exercised a beneficial influence over them. Laurence Surius, who was a year younger and had been influenced by the new doctrines, gives testimony of this. He was led back to the practice of the true religion by the courage and example of Peter Canisius. Soon after his conversion he entered the Carthusian Monastery at Cologne. In this way Peter Canisius spent his time at the University, where he devoted himself to the study of civil and canon law. Having been proclaimed a Doctor of Philosophy on May 25th, 1540, Peter Canisius soon afterwards returned to Nymwegen. His father destined for him a brilliant career in the world. It was in accordance with his father's wishes that the young student had followed the lectures in canon law at Cologne, and studied for some months in the University of Louvain. However, he had a distinct tendency for theological studies. In the month of February, 1540, two days after the entry of his friend Surius into the Carthusian Monastery, he made a vow of perpetual chastity. At that time his father recommended him a

suitable marriage from every point of view;
but Peter Canisius respectfully declined,
saying that he wished to give himself entirely
to the service of God.   In the meantime
he returned to Cologne and began to study
theology.

About this time the Society of Jesus was
founded by St. Ignatius, and received the
definite approval of the Holy See.   One of
the first companions of St. Ignatius, Blessed
Peter Faber, went to Mainz in the beginning
of the year 1543, and preached there with
great success.   Peter Canisius determined to
go and consult him, having in mind, perhaps,
the two-fold prediction which had been
made to him some years previously.   " I
remember," he relates in his *Testament*,
" the prophecies of a saintly widow, who,
during her life and at her death, was remarkable for her piety.   By Divine revelation
she told me that God would raise up a new
Order of simple and faithful priests, and that
I was one day to join this Order.   But at
that time no one spoke of the religious order
which is now known by the name of the
Jesuits. . . . Likewise a virgin, equally pious
and wise, from Brabant, foretold to me,
amongst other things, that my works and

writings would one day be useful to the Church of God."

Peter Canisius made a retreat, following the spiritual exercises of St. Ignatius, under the direction of Blessed Peter Faber. This retreat lasted thirty days; but Peter Canisius did not wait until the end in order to come to a decision concerning his vocation. In the second week he made a vow to enter the Society of Jesus. It is contained in the following words : " In the year 1543, on the 8th May, the Feast of the Apparition of St. Michael, the day of my birth, after full deliberation, I, Peter Canisius, make this vow to God Almighty, the Blessed Virgin Mary, St. Michael the Archangel, and all the Saints, to give my allegiance from this moment to the Society of Jesus. . . . As a perpetual momento I sign this vow with my name and I intend also to receive Holy Communion."

Having been admitted to the novitiate by Blessed Peter Faber, Peter Canisius returned to Cologne to continue his studies. At the same time he devoted himself to different works of charity and to teaching the catechism. During the Christmas festivities of the year 1543 news was brought from

Nymwegen that James Kanis was seriously ill, and wished to see his son. Peter Canisius departed immediately and only arrived in time to see his old father before his death. The sorrow of the young novice was manifested by the long and fervent prayers which he said for the soul of his deceased father. These prayers were rewarded by God ; for from that time Peter Canisius had the assurance that the salvation of his parents was beyond doubt. He distributed the larger portion of his wealth to the poor, and the remainder he devoted to the needs of his brethren in religion at Cologne.

The little community increased to nine members and was under the direction of Blessed Peter Faber. While the Superior devoted himself to preaching, the novices spent their leisure, after their study and spiritual exercises, in visiting the sick, distributing alms to the poor, and in reclaiming sinners, especially those who had gone astray in error. This activity was the reason why the novices were persecuted, and for this reason they had to separate for a time. An attempt was made to induce Peter Canisius to leave his brethren by offering to him a more favourable position in the Church of

St. Géréon, or at the Cathedral. He refused and continued with more zeal than ever in his charitable works. When circumstances became more favourable, the community was reunited.

Peter Canisius was ordained Deacon in December, 1544. He was given the task of commenting on the Gospel of St. Matthew on feast days at the College Du Mont. Having become a Bachelor in Holy Scripture, he explained the Epistles of St. Paul, and took part in discussions on the same subject in the presence of the professors of the University. He was held in such esteem by the latter that his Superiors were approached with a view to keeping him at Cologne. At that time there was a rumour that the young Jesuit had to leave the town to go to Louvain. An opportunity was afforded him at that time of expressing his affection for Cologne and its inhabitants. " If obedience," he affirms, " does not oblige me to leave this place, I am ready to spend for holy Cologne my poor body, my feeble intelligence, all my time, my studies, in one word, my being and all that belongs to me."

It was not, however, till 1547 that he was obliged to terminate completely his residence

in Cologne. In 1545 he made several journeys;
nevertheless he was afforded an opportunity
of seeing his old master, van Esch. In 1546
he visited Nymwegen to attend to family
business, and in the same year he was
ordained priest, on the 12th June, at Cologne.
On the following day, the Feast of Pentecost,
he celebrated his first Mass in the Church
of the Canonesses of St. Augustine. After
his ordination Peter Canisius devoted himself
more especially to preaching. It was at this
time that he edited the works of St. Cyril of
Alexandria and St. Leo the Great. His zeal
and the zeal of his companions filled St.
Ignatius with joy, who encouraged them by
his letters.

In the month of December, 1545, an important Council was held at Trent. Cardinal
Otho Truchsess, Bishop of Augsburg, com-
missioned Peter Canisius to represent him.
He arrived in Trent in February, 1547, when
the discussions were being held concerning
the Sacraments of Baptism and Confirmation.
When the Council was transferred to Bologna,
Peter Canisius went there. His stay, however, was a short one; for he was summoned
to Rome by the Founder of the Society of
Jesus. In the beginning of September, 1547,

he arrived at the Eternal City, where he was welcomed with joy by St. Ignatius, who wished personally to examine his dispositions. St. Ignatius at first gave him orders to carry out the humblest duties in the community, to beg from door to door, and to attend the sick in the hospitals. All these duties were faithfully performed ; for Peter Canisius had practised complete self-renunciation for many years. Thus, when he was asked whether he was willing to go to Sicily, he replied without hesitation : " I am indifferent whether I go to Sicily or to India or to any other part of the globe, which is assigned to me by obedience. If I am sent to Sicily, I shall willingly perform all duties, those of porter, cook, gardener, or professor. . . . I make a vow of leaving to my Superior the government of my soul and body."

On March 18th, 1547, Peter Canisius left Rome for Messina, where he was to become a professor in the first college which the Society founded in Sicily. A stay of a few days in Naples was spent in teaching catechism and in visiting the sick. In Messina Peter Canisius, besides teaching, devoted himself to the ministry, preached in Italian, and exercised a beneficial apostolate among the

students of the college. Many of the latter
took the resolution of joining the Society of
Jesus. However, he did not stay long in
Sicily. A larger field was to be assigned to
him for his activities by Divine Providence.
He was called to Rome to make his solemn
profession. On September 2nd, 1549, he
was presented to Pope Paul III. After the
audience Peter Canisius went into the Basilica
of St. Peter to pray at the altar of SS. Peter
and Paul, to beg their blessing on the mission
which had been entrusted to him of defend-
ing the Catholic faith in Germany. On this
day and two days afterwards, in the same
Basilica, he was the recipient of remarkable
favours from God, which he describes as
follows : " I was kneeling before the altar
of the Apostles SS. Peter and Paul when a
new benefit was bestowed upon me by the
sending of an angel to instruct and to aid
me. . . . . In the company of this blessed
spirit I advanced towards the altar and
then knelt down. . . . At that moment, O
Divine Redeemer, Thou didst open to me
Thy adorable Heart and didst grant me
to look into It. Thou didst invite me to
draw from thence the waters of salvation
and to drink of Thy sacred founts. With

what ardour I desired to be filled with Thy
love, hope, and faith ! What desires I had
for poverty, chastity, and obedience! Then
bringing my lips to Thy Sacred Heart, I
desired to drink from this source and Thou
promised me, O Saviour, to cover my poor
soul with the triple garment of peace,
charity, and constancy."

Such was the apparition of the Sacred
Heart, which is recalled by the historians
of Peter Canisius and by Pope Pius X in a
letter addressed to the College of Innsbruck.
Canisius himself preserved a lively remem-
brance of it throughout his life. It is
recorded that on his deathbed he held in
his hands a copy of the prayers which he
was wont to say. It is also related that by
means of these prayers he offered his day to
the Sacred Heart of Jesus. On September
4th, 1549, during Mass, which was celebrated
by St. Ignatius in the little Church of Maria
della Strada, Peter Canisius made his final
vows. Peter Canisius and the two Jesuits
who were to accompany him to Germany
were not Doctors of Divinity. Consequently,
all three went to Bologna, where they
successfully passed the examination for the
same degree on October 4th, the Feast of

St. Francis of Assisi. Later Peter Canisius
relates that on this occasion he took care
to invoke the protection of St. Francis
and also of St. Dominic, at whose tomb he
had prayed fervently.

CHAPTER IV

It was at the request of the Duke of Bavaria
and by the invitation of Pope Paul III that
St. Ignatius sent Peter Canisius and two
other Jesuits as Professors to Ingolstadt.
They were received there with great honour
on November 13th, 1549, and immediately
devoted themselves to their work, the
magnitude of which may be ascertained by
the following passage of a letter written
by St. Peter Canisius : " The masters of
good and solid doctrine are few in number
here and are not anxious to make their
students better. Most of the professors have
little standing from the point of view of
science. In their teaching they are less
concerned with the truths of the Gospel
than with doctrines favouring the passions.
Among them are secret or open heretics,
who spread, more or less openly, the poison
of error in the minds of their students. . . .
Left to themselves and without guidance,

young men have no love for study and no desire to advance in science. False doctrine and immorality have been spread among the people. The faithful are no longer Catholics except in name ; they live without giving a thought to their souls and a future life ; they despise the authority of their pastors and of the Church. . . . I write this in order to arouse your charity to pray that grace may abound more where sin has already abounded."

Peter Canisius and his companions undertook this work of reforming morals and thought which was to be the great endeavour of his life. Not content with giving his lectures in theology, he endeavoured by special lessons to make good the lack of preparation of many of his students. He was especially concerned with their souls, and succeeded in leading many back to the practice of piety. Having been appointed Rector of the University, he displayed great zeal in introducing necessary reforms. Thus he forbade the sale of works which were dangerous for faith or morals. The position of Vice-Chancellor was offered to him after his tenure of the office of Rector. He accepted it only for a specified time and on condition of not benefitting by the emoluments attached to the same.

In the midst of his occupations at the University, Peter Canisius did not forget the people of Ingolstadt. Sermons and services were badly attended at that time. He began to teach the children the catechism and also how to pray. He preached in different churches, which soon were not large enough to contain the crowds desirous of hearing him. The Holy Sacrifice of the Mass, which was held in small esteem and almost neglected, regained its place of honour in the religious life of the people. Peter Canisius, on coming down from the pulpit, used to kneel at the foot of the altar, reciting aloud prayers which were suitable to the needs of his hearers, and in which his listeners soon acquired the habit of joining. Such zeal proved to the inhabitants of Ingolstadt how true was the testimony given to Peter Canisius and his two companions by the Rector of the University soon after their arrival. In one word it is summed up as follows : " Their profound knowledge of the sacred sciences and the holiness of their lives have surpassed all expectations." Thus, when St. Ignatius determined to recall Peter

Canisius, to send him to Vienna, the news was received with very great regret. In order to escape the demonstration of sympathy organised by the University, Peter Canisius and his companions secretly left the town on the 9th March, 1552.

The Jesuits had been established for some time in Vienna at the request of King Ferdinand when Peter Canisius arrived. He began by teaching in the College which had just been opened. Afterwards he occupied a professorial chair at the University. He soon observed that the Catholic religion was more neglected in this place than in Ingolstadt. Only one-tenth of the population had been preserved from error or indifference. A large number of the parishes were deprived of pastors. The first task of Peter Canisius was to find suitable candidates for the priesthood. In addition to the College already in existence, Peter Canisius founded a Seminary for students in theology. In this College St. Stanislaus Kostka studied seventeen years later. About this time the German College was commenced in Rome through the efforts of St. Ignatius. Peter Canisius also had a share in this work, which was destined to provide a well-equipped clergy for the countries of Central Europe. In the meantime the Jesuits living in Vienna supplied the want of priests. Peter Canisius was able to combine teaching with all the duties of the ministry, namely, preaching in convents and different churches in the town, where his word and example produced the same excellent results as in Ingoldstadt ; evangelising the parishes in the country, where he succeeded in leading back to the practice of the Catholic religion a large number of the faithful ; visiting prisoners who, as he said, "were doubly unhappy because they were captives in body and soul"; and visiting the sick in their homes or in hospitals, for whose benefit he printed a special leaflet of prayers. The plague soon afterwards broke out in Vienna, having devastated the country. This outbreak only caused him to be more devoted and indefatigable than ever.

He was appointed Court preacher ; but this new honour did not prevent him from becoming all things to all men. He took advantage of a Jubilee granted by the Pope to the whole kingdom to explain and defend the doctrine of the Church on Indulgences. He took care to give special instructions to

the people on this point, which was so much
debated and so often misunderstood at that
time. The words of St. Paul—" Preach the
word ; be instant in season, out of season,
reprove, entreat, rebuke in all patience and
doctrine " (2 Timothy iv. 1)—indicate some
of the qualities of a good Bishop, but they
also characterise the ministry of Peter
Canisius at Vienna. The holy Jesuit, in
spite of his youth—he was then thirty-two
years of age—was proposed to be Bishop
of this great city. The King, the Nuncio,
and the Pope himself were in agreement
on this matter ; but they could not overcome the opposition of St. Ignatius, who
from the beginning of the foundation of
his Order had made the inflexible rule that
Jesuits were not to accept ecclesiastical
dignities. However, he allowed Peter
Canisius to undertake the administration
of the diocese for one year only, and on
the condition of receiving none of the
emoluments.

While the business was being negotiated,
Peter Canisius commenced the most popular
work of his life, namely, his *Catechism*.
His large Catechism appeared in April, 1555,
in one volume, in octavo, containing one

hundred and ninety-three pages, without the name of the author, and without any mention of place or date, adorned with three wood engravings and a beautiful title page in red and black : *Summa Doctrinae christianae per quaestiones tradita et in usum christianae pueritiae nunc primum edita* (" Summary of Christian Doctrine in the form of Questions and Answers for the Use of Catholic Youth, now published for the first time"). It comprised two hundred and eleven questions and answers, the question and answer sometimes filling four or five pages.

It was written in Latin ; but Latin at that time was not a dead language. It was spoken by cultivated men and students, to whom the new catechism was addressed. By giving it the name of *Summa* (Summary), Peter Canisius followed the tradition which arose in the Middle Ages of thus naming every text-book complete in one branch of knowledge. A German translation appeared in the next year, 1556, followed by many other editions.

Peter Canisius reduces Christian Doctrine to two general ideas, namely, wisdom and justice, in accordance with the words of the Book of Ecclesiasticus : " Son, if thou desire wisdom, keep justice, and God will give her to thee." (Chap. i. 33.) Wisdom comprises four chapters : 1. Faith and the Creed. 2. Hope and the Lord's Prayer. 3. Charity and the Decalogue, to which are joined the Commandments of the Church and the Church herself. 4. The Sacraments. The second part, namely, Justice, fills the fifth and last chapter ; Justice consists in fleeing from evil and in doing good. Here Peter Canisius explains sin, good works, virtues, the gifts and fruits of the Holy Ghost, the Evangelical Counsels, and the four last ends—death, judgment, hell, and heaven.

The doctrines which were not disputed at that time by Protestants, namely, the existence of God, the Divinity of Christ, the immortality of the soul, the authority of Scripture, the eternal punishment of hell, are briefly but concisely set forth. On the contrary, truths which were attacked by the reformers are taught at great length and defended by numerous quotations from Scripture and the Fathers. The text of the Catechism is a tissue of words of the Gospels and other books of Holy Scripture, so that St. Peter Canisius expounds clearly the teaching of Our Lord Jesus Christ.

In the first edition there are one thousand one hundred and one references to the Bible, and four hundred references to the Fathers, given in the margin ; but the revised edition of 1566 contains two thousand references to Holy Scripture and one thousand two hundred references to the Fathers, likewise given in the margin. In 1569 Father de Buys (Busaeus), S.J., a fellow-countryman of Peter Canisius, published under his direction the *Opus catechisticum*, which is the edition of the large Catechism issued in 1566 with the quotations from Scripture and the Fathers printed in full. This work is often called the Catechism of Theologians. Pope Leo XIII, in his Encyclical of August 1st, 1897, praises the Catechism of Peter Canisius as "world famous, distinguished by its magnificent style and worthy of the pen of a Father of the Church."

Pope Leo XIII continues as follows : "Less voluminous, but no less useful were the two very celebrated Catechisms which St. Peter Canisius wrote for not so well informed people ; the one to teach the elements of religion to children, the other to instruct youth who had already begun to study literature. These two works became

so popular amongst Catholics that they
were used by men appointed to teach the
principles of truth. Not only were they
employed in the schools to impart the milk
of doctrine, but they were also publicly
explained in the churches. Thus, for three
centuries, Canisius was regarded as the
master of the Catholics of Germany, and in
the vernacular 'knowing Canisius' and 'keeping the Christian truth' were synonymous
expressions." Thus besides the large Catechism, Peter Canisius was the author of the
middle-sized or intermediate Catechism and
the small Catechism.

The Catechism of Peter Canisius, in its
different forms, has been published hundreds
of times and translated into almost all the
European languages, even to our own times.
In 1615 there were Ethiopian, Japanese
and Hindu versions. Few books have had
such a great circulation and have produced
such remarkable results. It was the purpose
of the author, as he himself says, " to uplift
the fallen and to guide in the right road
those who have strayed." It was, however,
due to his tact that he was successful,
because he made no reference to opponents
of the Church. In the work are to be found

numerous quotations of Holy Scripture, and from the Fathers of the Church. These quotations were used to illustrate the truths and practices of the Catholic religion. They always led to their centre, Jesus Christ ; for Peter Canisius says : " We should obey Christ, our chief, and suffer with Him in order to be glorified with Him." To suffer with Christ was, indeed, the lot of Peter Canisius. He met with opposition, not only from Protestants, but also from Catholics who were offended by his frankness and perfect orthodoxy. At his request St. Ignatius, from the year 1553, commanded all the priests of the Society of Jesus to offer the Holy Sacrifice of the Mass, once a month, for the spiritual needs of the countries of Central Europe. Peter Canisius himself was a man of prayer. The pictures which represent him telling his beads manifest the principal secret of his success and the holiness of his life.

Peter Canisius wrote some months after his departure for Prague, where the Jesuits were to found a college, the following words : " Alas ! there has been no Bishop in Bohemia for one hundred years. May God give us the grace to come to the assistance of this portion of His Kingdom, to build again His temples and to lead back the wandering sheep to their Supreme Pastor. I should wish that all the Fathers who have been sent to found this college should possess patience and ardent zeal, not for discussion but for suffering, and to edify by their example rather than by their word, so that having sown in tears they may reap in joy." Having arrived at Prague in the month of July, 1555, he made arrangements for the foundation of the College. Canisius acted with much prudence and charity. While this business was taken in hand, he applied himself to preaching and explaining the Catechism, at the same time being careful to avoid any attacks upon Protestants, who were very numerous in the country. The Dominicans handed over their convent of St. Clement to be converted into a college. The building was uncomfortable ; rain and snow penetrated the roof ; yet provision was made in the best possible way for class-rooms. Twelve Jesuits who arrived from Rome had difficulty in finding the necessaries of life during the first month. In addition persecution began, especially when many pupils came to the new school. One day, during Mass, Peter Canisius, in his own phrase, "was greeted by a stone that was thrown against the window of the church."

The Jesuits, by their patience and charity, eventually disarmed their adversaries, many of whom entrusted to them the education of their children. At the same time that the College of Prague was founded, Peter Canisius commenced the College of Ingolstadt. During his stay in this city, in the month of June, 1556, word was brought that he had been appointed Provincial of the South German Province of the Society of Jesus, with authority over the Houses of the Jesuits then in existence or about to be established in Austria, Bohemia, and in Germany properly so-called. The humble Jesuit, who was then scarcely thirty-five years of age, immediately wrote to St. Ignatius : " Willingly I sacrifice my life for the benefit of the Company, and for the welfare of my brethren ; but I am entirely lacking in tact, prudence and decision, which is necessary for the govern-ment of others. My temper is hasty and fiery, and my inexperience renders me quite unfit for this position. May God grant you to penetrate into the depth of my soul and see my misery. In the midst of my manifold occupations I have lost everything that constitutes a religious. If you knew me, you would have pity on me and help me by your prayers, for which I ask in all humility." In his reply St. Ignatius appealed to the spirit of submission of Peter Canisius. He exhorted him to place all his confidence in the grace of God, which is never wanting to obedient souls.

The appointment of the Provincial of the South German Province was one of the last important acts of the Founder of the Society of Jesus. Some weeks afterwards, on the 31st July, 1556, St. Ignatius died at Rome. Peter Canisius received this news with great sorrow, but also in the spirit of faith. He wrote as follows concerning St. Ignatius : " He is so happy, because he has gone to his heavenly fatherland. He has lived in such a manner that death cannot be a misfortune for him. From the height of heaven he will take more interest in us than he could here below. May I obtain by his intercession a slight resemblance to his religious spirit."

CHAPTER V

THE task which St. Ignatius had imposed
before his death on Peter Canisius was
difficult. The situation in Austria and
Germany from the point of view of religion
required prompt and energetic measures.
For more than thirty years these countries
were very much divided. Differences of
doctrine between Protestants and Catholics
had given rise to fierce political struggles.
The Emperor and other Princes, as well as
Bishops, sought to safeguard their temporal
interests, and in so doing made regrettable
concessions. This frame of mind is visible
in the Diet of Ratisbon, summoned by King
Ferdinand. Upon the invitation of this
prince, Peter Canisius accompanied thither
one of the most distinguished prelates of
the time, Cardinal Otho Truchsess. He
preached in the Cathedral during almost a
whole winter, 1556 to 1557, with considerable
success.

In the meetings of the Diet the Lutheran Princes demanded a conference in which Catholic theologians and leaders of the reformers should meet and discuss. In order to win the support of the Protestants in the struggle against the Turks, King Ferdinand acceded to their request and gave permission for a conference to take place at Worms. Six theologians were appointed to uphold Catholic doctrine. Peter Canisius was one of the first to be chosen, notwithstanding the fact that he was openly opposed to this discussion. He said that he had " learned by experience that conferences on doctrine only aggravated the evil ; time was lost in disputes without results. Heated discussions took place ; the chasm which separated Catholics from Dissentients was widened. . . . With my lack of talent, my incapability and insufficiency, I should like to flee from here and go away to beg in the Indies, rather than take part in these dangerous disputes ; but God manifests His Will by my Superior. Once I know this Will I shall be without fear, even though I am confronted with a host of enemies. All my strength and all my confidence arise from obedience, and throughout the whole of my life I shall look upon myself in the house of God as none other than a beast of burden."

His Superiors, as well as Pope Paul IV, expressed their wish that Peter Canisius should take part in the conference. He obeyed ; but what he had foreseen was the result. No understanding was reached on the programme for discussion at Worms. The Protestants were divided amongst themselves. Some left the town, and their departure provided a reason for ending the discussion. "Perhaps a consequence will be," wrote Peter Canisius, "that Princes will no longer desire conferences which remedy nothing. They will then have recourse to restore the Catholic religion through the only available means, namely, a Council. This is the desire of many people whose science equals their piety. Several hope to obtain it from the reigning Pontiff ; yet there are many who always have fears." The reform of the Church by the Church, a Catholic reformation, was the end to be obtained in the view of Peter Canisius. This was the request which he made courageously to the ecclesiastical and civil authorities who asked his advice. In this task several sought the aid of the courageous Provincial.

It is difficult to describe, even briefly, all the journeys which he undertook in Germany, Bavaria, Austria and Italy at this time. At Cologne he was welcomed with the greatest honour. When he left the Cathedral, where he had preached in the presence of three thousand people, he was escorted as though he were an emperor or a king. At Strasbourg he made arrangements for the foundation of a college, and he received from the Chapter of the Cathedral among other gifts a relic of St. Polycarp, which is still to be seen in one of the reliquaries of the Church of St. Michael in Fribourg. At Dillingen he was the guest of Cardinal Truchsess, Bishop of Augsburg, who showed his respect by washing his feet. This great Bishop loved Peter Canisius very much. This love was returned by the latter, but sometimes in an unexpected manner. Thus, having learned that the Cardinal made several visits to the court of the Emperor, or even to Rome, where the Pope willingly consulted him, he wrote to remind him of the duty of residence : "At Augsburg many people look forward to the return of Your Highness, and this for very good reasons. Things are going much worse than you can imagine in Rome, and by delay the conscience of the Bishop is loaded with great responsibility. I cannot understand how Your Highness can sleep calmly when so many souls are perishing, and while the shepherds themselves risk such great danger. May Your Highness pardon me for speaking so openly, because I love Your Eminence Cardinal Otho, and my gratitude for so many benefits received from you imposes this duty upon me." Such frankness did not displease the prelate. On the contrary, he held the holy Jesuit in greater esteem.

One day, during the month of May, 1558, two religious knocked at the door of the College of the Jesuits in Loretto, Italy, and asked for hospitality. The porter asked for the letter or the permission signed by their Superior. The eldest replied that he had no letter, since he himself was the Superior of the South German Province. " It is no use saying that," replied the Brother, " it is the first credential that a newcomer must present. You shall not come in." The Brother retired, leaving the two travellers at the door. They waited patiently for nearly an hour, when at last one of the Fathers of the College, on his return from the church, met them and learnt with astonishment that one of the religious was Peter Canisius. The Rector was notified and immediately sought to excuse the unfortunate porter, who was all in confusion. " I have nothing to pardon ; he has only done his duty," Peter Canisius replied with a smile.

He went to Rome ; for the Provincial of the South German Province had to take part in the election of a General of the Society of Jesus, which had been postponed for two years. He was given the duty of delivering an address, before the ballot, to the assembled Jesuits. They chose as their General, Father Laynez, who had exercised the duties of Vicar-General since the death of St. Ignatius. Some days afterwards the Jesuits in Rome were received in solemn audience by Pope Paul IV. In the beginning of September Peter Canisius set out for his Province, and immediately went to Poland to help the Nuncio of the Pope with his advice. For three months he stayed in this country, which had been largely won over to

Protestantism. During his stay he revived the courage of the faithful by his exhortations, writings, and the example of his virtues.

The weakness of Catholic princes and the lack of Catholic clergy were a great sorrow to him. Consequently he wrote as follows : " God gives me to understand the importance of the vow made by the members of the Society of Jesus to devote themselves freely and entirely to souls in every place, at every time, without counting the cost, placing all their confidence in the infinite goodness of Jesus Christ. . . . I see clearly the importance of devoting oneself especially to the defence of the Holy See in these unhappy times." This supernatural way of thinking, which Peter Canisius wished his brethren to possess, he also endeavoured to develop within himself, especially by the practice of obedience and humility. The following is an example. When he was about to leave Poland he went to see the Emperor Ferdinand. The latter made him promise not to accept any other mission, and to keep himself in reserve for the Diet, which was about to be held at Augsburg. After Peter Canisius had made this promise, he had some scruples and reproached himself for not having consulted his Superiors before giving his pledge. He wrote to Father Laynez, giving him an account of what had happened, and asked him to give him a penance. Then he added : " I am in Poland and I shall stay there, being persuaded that my toil, rendered acceptable by obedience, will be blessed by Our Saviour, because we belong to Him everywhere and always." It does not appear that the General of the Society thought this was an occasion to impose a penance which had been asked with so much humility ; but he allowed Peter Canisius to reply to the invitation of the Emperor and to leave Poland to go to Augsburg.

It is necessary, here, to describe briefly the manner in which he fulfilled his duties as Provincial. These duties alone were sufficient to occupy a man of ordinary energy. It was not merely a question of watching over and developing houses already in existence ; but it was also necessary to erect new ones ; for on all sides requests were made for Jesuits as professors or preachers. Peter Canisius then had to undertake numerous journeys ; he had to display much energy, patience and tact in dealing either with Bishops, the secular and regular clergy, or with princes and cities. When he was appointed Provincial, Colleges in Vienna, Ingolstadt and Prague had just been organised by him. Soon after he founded Colleges in Munich, Innsbruck, and Dillingen. Later he paved the way for the foundations of other Colleges at Hall, Augsburg, and Würzburg. In his capacity as founder or Visitor of Colleges, Peter Canisius strove especially to make these schools centres of learning and piety. By his words, example, and letters he encouraged the masters and students, taking an active interest in their studies and their exercises of piety. He also devoted his attention to the financial condition of the Colleges, not shrinking from entering into details concerning manual labour or food.

In perusing the letters in which he rendered an account of his administration to the Superiors of his Order, one is not slow in admiring his supernatural insight, his concentration, and his practical mind. For example, writing to the Father-General, St. Francis Borgia, at the end of the year 1566, Peter Canisius described at great length clearly the problems of the College which had to be begun in Würzburg with very few Jesuits. Then he adds : " You will easily understand the difficulty of this new undertaking. There are many reasons to discourage us, if we consider only our slender means and our small number ; but the strength and grace of God have a power superior to human diligence and resources. You will see what is necessary to be done for the greater glory of God."

CHAPTER VI

APOSTLE OF AUGSBURG

WHEN Peter Canisius arrived at Augsburg, in March, 1559, an important Diet or assembly of the Lords of the Empire, both Catholic and Protestant, was being held under the direction of Ferdinand I. This Prince, who had learned at Vienna to value the knowledge and holiness of Peter Canisius, had in the previous year become the Chief of the Empire ; but his election had not been ratified by the Sovereign Pontiff. The situation was in consequence very difficult. Canisius felt this acutely. He realised how much depended on him to put an end to a disagreement, of which the enemies of the Church sought to take advantage. He prayed and caused prayers to be said ; he ordered fasts in the houses of his Province ; he put the Prince on his guard against the plans of violence which were suggested to him.

Ferdinand I, being thus encouraged, remained firmly attached to the Catholic religion and soon afterwards was recognised by Pope Pius IV.

In 1559 Peter Canisius began a very active ministry in the town of Augsburg, which was to last until 1566. From the moment of his arrival he preached in the Cathedral with such success that the Bishop, Canons and people, asked to have him appointed as ordinary preacher. They wrote to the General of the Society of Jesus—that by allowing one of his subjects, whose knowledge and holiness were known throughout Germany, to remain in Augsburg, he was performing an action which was very pleasing to God and very useful to the Church. Father Laynez gave his consent, and the new preacher presented himself on the 24th June, the Feast of the Nativity of St. John the Baptist. He eulogised his predecessor and humbly stated that he had neither his eloquence nor his knowledge, and that he placed himself entirely at the disposal of those who, in addition to his instructions, had need of longer explanations and encouragement.

The sermons preached by Peter Canisius at Augsburg number hundreds, and deal with all kinds of subjects, but especially

with those which were most disputed by
Catholics and Protestants, for example, the
question of Indulgences. Besides, the
preacher attacked with much energy the
vices and disorders of his age, which were
so harmful from the moral point of view.
Not satisfied with clearly setting forth his
subjects by quotations from Holy Scripture
and the Fathers of the Church, he had
recourse to the great power of prayer in
order to touch hearts more efficaciously.
He prayed and he caused prayers to be said
before and after the sermon ; he asked his
hearers to sing popular hymns ; he mingled
fervent invocations with his preaching.
Moreover the example of his holy life, the
manifestation of his virtues and especially
of his charity, completed his teaching. It
was common knowledge that Peter Canisius
regularly heard Confessions, visited the sick,
and interested himself in poor students,
even to the extent of begging for them.
These works of charity were only interrupted
by discharging his duties as Provincial.

God rewarded the efforts of the holy
Jesuit. The large town of Augsburg, which
had been infected by the new doctrines,
scarcely contained eight thousand Catholics

out of twenty-four thousand inhabitants, when Peter Canisius was appointed preacher at the Cathedral. These Catholics were lukewarm or timid. At the most fifty followed the exercises of Lent or assisted in the procession of the Feast of Corpus Christi. Soon their devotion was enkindled and numerous conversions were the result. Contemporaries describe the religious revival as follows[1]:—

" Not for one hundred years has there been seen in Augsburg so much zeal or enthusiasm for the practice of religion as in our day, in order to gain the Indulgences granted by the Pope. The eagerness of the people in going to Confession, in receiving Holy Communion, and in taking part in processions has been marvellous. If Peter Canisius remains with us he will do untold good. . . . Many of the faithful go to Confession and receive Holy Communion even every week. Many kneel on the bare ground during the entire Mass. The Confraternities of the Rosary flourish again ; pilgrimages, even on bare foot, receive honourable recognition."

[1] These sentences are selected as being typical from letters received by Cardinal Truchsess when he was absent from his episcopal city of Augsburg. *Saint Pierre Canisius*, by E. Morand ; Fribourg, 1925, p. 50. *Quatrième Centenaire de la naissance du Bienheureux Pierre Canisius* ; Fribourg, 1923, p. III.

Yet like all true apostles, Peter Canisius encountered contradictions and trials at Augsburg. Some thought that his supernatural zeal was exaggerated. In spite of criticisms and persecutions he continued his course of sermons until 1566. Moreover, he was continually encouraged by his friend the Bishop of Augsburg. Pope Pius IV himself wrote to him in the month of March, 1561, a letter of congratulation, in which the following words are found : " We have been informed of the cleverness, zeal, and charity you have employed in bringing back to the way of salvation a large number of the souls snatched from the true religion. These tidings have caused us very much consolation. Continue, my dear son, as you have begun, and strive to win to God as many souls as you can. Be devoted to this holy apostolate, and do not recoil from any sacrifice in the assurance that you are to receive the reward of good and faithful servants."

It is written in the Book of Proverbs, that, " the fear of the Lord is the lesson of wisdom : and humility goeth before glory " (Chap. xv. 33). This saying is fulfilled many times in the case of Peter Canisius. He

6

never hesitated, when his Superiors had spoken, in undertaking a new burden of work and toil. In reality this obedience was rewarded with numerous successes which the holy Jesuit welcomed with his customary humility. Very often God visibly sustained the strength of His servant, who was often obliged to undertake important duties. Thus in 1561, when he was summoned to the Council of Trent, his interest was divided between the desire of helping the necessary work of Catholic reform and the will to continue his twofold duties as Provincial and preacher of the Cathedral at Augsburg. He wrote : " I am fully resigned to the decrees of the Divine mercy and to the orders of obedience. I have only one aim, to work, with the help of God, to further the interests of the Church." It was under the guidance of the Spirit of God that Peter Canisius arrived at Trent in the month of May, 1562. His arrival was marked by an event which many considered to be miraculous. Cardinal Hosius, who had earnestly asked for his assistance, was at the point of death. The visit of the holy Jesuit restored his strength, and some days afterwards he enjoyed his usual health.

Canisius took an active part in the work of the Council, which pursued slowly but surely its double end, namely, firstly, the defence of the Faith, by setting forth Catholic truth and pointing out contrary errors ; and secondly, the reform of morals, by issuing salutary decrees which were applicable to the pastors of the Church as well as to the simple faithful.   Peter Canisius was especially concerned with the questions about the *Index*, or the list of condemned books, and the Sacrament of the Holy Eucharist. He admired the freedom with which each one could open his mind. He said that " If our separated brethren were there, how many things they would learn ? " In the discussions he was conspicuous for his knowledge, his moderation, and also for his energy when occasion demanded it. " I have been called to speak at the Council," he wrote with simplicity. " It is said that I have done so with success. God has assisted me, thanks to the prayers of the Society. Let all the glory be given to Him ! "

Nevertheless the Catholics of Augsburg keenly felt his absence and cried out for his return.   " My good people of Augsburg clamour and lament," wrote the Bishop of the diocese, Cardinal Truchsess ; " their cries deafen my ears and pierce my heart. Why are these complaints made ? Undoubtedly because the enemy sows cockle in the midst of the good grain. I do not think it is possible to keep the master far from his disciples for long—the father separated from his children. The damage caused at Augsburg is greater than the good achieved at Trent." Consequently Peter Canisius left Trent, where he had stayed only for a few weeks ; but he continued to show his interest in the work of the Council by letters or reports, by the dispatch of books, as also by prayer and obtaining prayers for the success of the Catholic reformation. He happily intervened with the Emperor Ferdinand I, who, acting on bad advice, strove to impose dangerous concessions on the Church and had even summoned to Innsbruck an assembly of theologians to support him. When Peter Canisius was invited to this assembly he maintained with energy the rights of the Holy See.

The Papal Delegate to the Council wrote to Pope Pius IV : " Amongst these theologians we are fortunate in having Peter Canisius, a man of great piety and profound

knowledge. He is a powerful defender of
the Pope's authority." The courageous
Jesuit dared to represent to the Emperor
that he must distrust people who, under
the appearance of zeal, had for their object
" to revile the authority of the Apostolic
See, to restrain the power of the Roman
Pontiff, to sow discord in the Apostolical
Hierarchy, and to put themselves in opposition to the Church, which was represented
at Trent by the *élite* of the Doctors of
Christendom and was assisted by the infallible
light of the Holy Ghost."

Ferdinand I was obliged to withdraw his
demands. Later, in connection with the
question which was then very much discussed,
namely, Communion under two kinds, he
was able to declare the energy and indepen-
dence with which Peter Canisius upheld
the interest of the Catholic faith. He showed
his displeasure by marked coldness and
reserve towards him. The holy Jesuit undoubtedly felt interiorly this change in the
attitude of a Prince, who, on so many other
occasions, was pious, zealous and devoted to
the Catholic Church ; but in this instance,
as always, he set the cause of the Church
above human considerations. " I have no

understanding whatever of these human politics," he said. " I know well that to speak the truth stirs up hatred ; but this will not be a reason for me to keep silence. The time has come loudly to proclaim the cause of the Church and to present an unconquerable resistance to those who attack its rights."

CHAPTER VII

It is customary for a Nuncio, a Legate, a Bishop, or a Cardinal to be entrusted by the Holy See with an important mission to the Governments of nations. Why did the Sovereign Pontiff deem it expedient, in 1565, to make an exception to this rule, by making a humble Jesuit his representative to a certain number of Bishops, Princes and Towns of Germany ? The reason was because no one enjoyed in these countries such influence as Peter Canisius. When he was called to Rome to take part in the election of a Superior-General of his Order, the Cardinal of Augsburg wrote to St. Francis Borgia, who was going to be appointed General of the Jesuits some months afterwards : "Although this journey does not appear to me to be disinterested, I think that I must explain to you the state of Germany. The Catholic Princes have amongst them few theologians imbued with sound doctrine, right sense, and ardent zeal

79

who can give advice ; but Peter Canisius, by
his worth and knowledge, has no equal in
this respect. . . . In the Diet which is about
to be opened, very important questions will
have to be dealt with and defined. Peter
Canisius, be assured, thanks to the high
esteem and the great reputation which he
enjoys with Princes, will be able to give them
salutary advice and counsel. By the sound-
ness of his doctrine, by his wisdom, by his
preaching and the example of a holy life,
he works with success in the service of God
and the Church."

Pope Pius IV knew all these things. He
knew also the part which had been taken
by Peter Canisius in the deliberations of
the Council of Trent, and how he had
always worked in perfect union with the
Holy See to uphold the integrity of the
Catholic Faith. This is the reason why,
on September 19th, 1565, Peter Canisius left
Rome with the title of Apostolic Delegate
and the mission of hastening the application
of the decrees of the Council in one part of
Germany. This was a delicate mission ; for
the severe measures taken by the Church to
develop religious instruction and to reform
morals were not pleasing to all ; and in some

countries there were refusals to adopt them.
It was necessary then to overcome the
opposition of some, to come to the assistance
of the apathy of others, and to sustain
courageous Bishops who had taken the work
in hand. This work was accomplished by
Peter Canisius. He wrote from Dillingen
to St. Francis Borgia and recommended
himself to his prayers and to those of his
brethren. Then he set out on his journey
with his usual companion. The first town
he visited was Würzburg, where the Bishop
earnestly asked him to found a Jesuit College
in his diocese.

In the diocese of Mainz there was the
question of the organisation of a Seminary,
in accordance with the decrees of the Council
of Trent. In the diocese of Treves the
endowment of a college already existing
was dealt with. Canisius only passed through
Cologne ; thence he went to spend a few
days in his native town. The inhabitants of
Nymwegen gave their distinguished fellow-
countryman a rousing reception. Peter
Canisius accepted the hospitality of his
brother-in-law, Councillor Godefroid van
Triest, who later became Burgomaster. On
the day of his arrival he visited the Latin

school where he had made his first literary studies, and he spoke in Latin to the pupils and their parents. In the Church of St. Stephen, where he had prayed as a child, he preached on two different occasion before thousands of people and heard numerous confessions.

Interested in the spiritual welfare of his family, he asked to see them individually, namely, his brethren, his sister and their children. He became acquainted with their reading and their practices of piety and exhorted them to remain steadfast in the faith of their ancestors. All wished to receive him at least once in their homes. Not being able to satisfy them, he asked them to have a repast in the hotel of the town. In this way they shared a common table, and the poor benefited in like manner. This day of farewell in accordance with the wish of Peter Canisius was begun by the celebration of Holy Mass and the reception of Holy Communion. The example of charity given by the family of Peter Canisius on this occasion has never been forgotten in Nymwegen. On the occasion of the celebration of the third centenary of the birth of Peter Canisius the poor were invited to High Mass which was followed by a repast in common. Having thus instructed and edified his fellow-countrymen, Peter Canisius left Nymwegen which he was destined not to see again. Nevertheless he took an interest in his Catholic fellow-citizens, who later underwent a religious persecution. Several of his letters to his family have been preserved, in which he exhorts his brothers and sisters to give their children a Catholic education and insists particularly on the frequent reception of the Sacraments.

The humble delegate of the Pope visited several towns and dioceses, encountering difficulties and eventually meeting with success. He was nowhere received more joyously than in Cologne. The clergy, Senate, University and people were glad to welcome the man whom they had known for his piety and devotion twenty years previously. The Pontifical decrees were heard respectfully and energetic measures were taken for the defence of religion. During this visit to Cologne Peter Canisius heard the news of the death of Pope Pius IV. At the beginning of 1566 he sent to the new Pope Pius V a report on the results of his mission. He was indeed exhausted in the fulfilment

of his duties. " God be thanked ! " he
wrote, " for granting me the strength to
undertake a journey lasting four months in
the midst of winter. Yet I feel depressed ;
for my strength has disappeared. May God's
will be done, and may He grant us to be
children of obedience in life and in death ! "

He was soon released from his delicate
mission, and the zealous Jesuit was sent to
the Diet of Augsburg to assist with his
advice Cardinal Commendone, Legate of the
Pope. He was thus able to resume the
course of his sermons in this large town.
The spacious Cathedral was too small to
contain the crowd of listeners, so that the
Empress and the Court asked to hear the
holy Jesuit in another church. Peter
Canisius was at the same time occupied with
the affairs that were considered by the Diet.
He used his influence to maintain the
good understanding between the Emperor
Maximilian II and the Holy See and to get
the decisions of the Council of Trent accepted
by the Princes assembled at Augsburg. The
last Lent when Peter Canisius preached in
the Cathedral at Augsburg was in the year
1566. His ministry which lasted seven years
was never forgotten. Fifty years afterwards

the Bishop of Augsburg wrote to the Pope that his Episcopal city was obliged to recognise the Venerable Peter Canisius as its Apostle.

In the same year, 1566, Peter Canisius resumed the government of his Province, which he had entrusted a year previously to his brother Father Theoderic, and which he himself retained till the year 1569. During these three years he made many journeys, preached, taught the catechism and was especially occupied with the different Houses placed under his direction. On one of these journeys he went to Innsbruck, where he had to deal with the foundation of the College of Hall. On the way he escaped death as by a miracle when he was crossing a river in flood. Father Rocca, who was his companion, was firmly persuaded that God had sent an angel to save the Father Provincial and allow him to work for some years more for the welfare of the Church in Germany by preaching, writing, and pious exhortation.

In the spring of 1568 Peter Canisius went to preach at Ellwangen, a town in the diocese of Augsburg. By his zeal he succeeded in leading back the clergy and the faithful to the practice of piety. The Bishop,

Cardinal Truchsess, made every effort to
ensure the success of this mission. He
himself taught catechism to the children;
he preached sermons; he received the poor
at his own table; he visited the sick
and took energetic measures to safeguard
purity of faith and morals. Singular to
relate, while Peter Canisius was still staying
at Ellwangen he heard that there was a
rumour at Würzburg that he had become
a Protestant. It was even stated that he
had publicly set forth the reasons for his
change in religion. Peter Canisius quietly
finished his sermons for Holy Week and
Easter. Then he went to Würzburg, and from
the pulpit of the Cathedral he energetically
denounced the calumny by declaring that
he was a son and a disciple of the Holy
Roman Church and its faithful defender.

On his return to Dillingen he soon had to
depart, because Cardinal Truchsess requested
him almost immediately to accompany him
to Rome. In Italy the two travellers stopped
at Ancona. Peter Canisius longed for retire-
ment and went to visit the beautiful Cathedral
which overlooks the town and the sea. He
was more than ever filled with the sense
of the greatness of God and of his own

weakness. Cardinal Truchsess and Peter Canisius continued their journey and shortly arrived at Loretto. The Bishop celebrated Pontifical Mass in the Basilica which shelters the Holy House of Nazareth, and the holy Jesuit preached in Latin on the reminiscences which this House recalls. He spoke with more unction, because at that time he was reflecting on his great work concerning the Blessed Virgin, in which a long chapter is devoted to the pilgrimage of Loretto.

At Rome Peter Canisius had several interviews with the Sovereign Pontiff, Pius V, in which he freely discussed the situation of the Church in Central Europe, and proposed different means for its improvement.

He also met St. Philip Neri. Naturally, he visited all the Houses of the Jesuits, in one of which he addressed the novices, among whom was St. Stanislaus Kotska. Peter Canisius had welcomed him at Dillingen the previous year, and sent him to Rome. As he delivered his discourse on the first day of the month, he asked his listeners to consider each month as the last month of their lives and to sanctify it particularly by purity of intention and the perfection of every action. St. Stanislaus Kotska was more impressed than anyone else by this instruction and announced his coming death. Two years later, on the morning of the Feast of the Assumption, he gave up his beautiful soul to God. After a stay of six months in Rome, Peter Canisius again resumed the rule of his Province. The following April, in 1569, he was released from his office of Provincial. On this occasion he wrote to the General of the Jesuits to thank him, to ask pardon for his omissions, and to request him to give him a penance for his faults. St. Francis Borgia replied by a letter of praise, in which he said : " I have no penance to give your Reverence for your faults, which you ask. Quite the contrary, I have the sure confidence that God will reward you generously for your untiring and fruitful labours which you have undergone in the administration of the Province."

CHAPTER VIII

REFUTATION OF THE CENTURIATORS OF MAGDEBURG

DILLINGEN is often referred to in connection with St. Peter Canisius. This town was the abode by choice of Cardinal Truchsess, the friend and protector of the holy Jesuit. Besides the Jesuits were in charge of a University there, and of a College which soon became prosperous. Here Peter Canisius went to live after being released from the charge of the South German Province. This is how the annual report of the College speaks of him : " Since Peter Canisius has ceased to be Provincial, he is in our midst giving an example of humility and most sincere charity. During the hours which he does not devote to his learned works, he teaches publicly Christian doctrine or the catechism and helps us to hear confessions." The holy works referred to are those which Peter Canisius had undertaken a year previously in obedience to the will of his Superiors and of the Pope.

The subject of the first was St. John the Baptist ; the theme of the second was the Blessed Virgin Mary ; and the remaining books dealt with Jesus Christ—the Redeemer of the World, St. Peter, St. Paul, St. John and St. James. These were a reply to the attacks of a certain number of Protestant authors, who had commenced to publish at Magdeburg a history of the Christian religion, in a sense hostile to the Catholic Church. Their work was divided into periods of one hundred years, or centuries ; hence is formed their name, " Centuriators " of Magdeburg.

The volume, written by St. Peter Canisius, on St. John the Baptist, appeared in 1571, and was entitled : " Commentary on the Changes in the Word of God—Book I, in which is described the Gospel Story of St. John the Baptist." Herein is to be found not only the history of the Precursor, but also a defence of Christian Doctrine on many points ; for example, he speaks of the use of Holy Scripture, fasting, good works, faith and the veneration of saints and relics. His book on the Blessed Virgin Mary, containing more than eight hundred pages, appeared in 1577, and is divided into five parts. The first part deals with the origin and Immaculate Conception of Mary, of her childhood and virtues ; in the second part he discourses upon her perfect virginity ; the third part concerns the Angelical Salutation and the errors made in its interpretation ; in the fourth part he explains the text of the Gospels which the opponents of the veneration of the Blessed Virgin Mary twist from their true sense ; lastly he speaks of the death of Our Lady, her Assumption, and the veneration which the Church has always given her.

These two works on St. John the Baptist and the Blessed Virgin Mary were composed in the midst of the toils of a very active ministry. His concentration is illustrated by the following story : In 1577, he preached during Lent at Landshut, where the Duke of Bavaria, William V, resided, and who held him in high esteem. He stayed in the Duke's house, together with his companion, who was his secretary. One day when he was dictating a portion of his work, his companion had to go into the town. Peter Canisius continued his deep thought. Soon afterwards, hearing someone enter, and thinking it was his companion, he resumed his dictation without lifting up his eyes. When his companion returned an hour later, he was astonished to find the Duke of Bavaria writing in his place. " Open your eyes and see who has taken down your dictation," he exclaimed. Peter Canisius flushed on seeing the Prince, and asked his pardon. " I have nothing to pardon," remarked Duke William. " I willingly consent to act as your secretary, deeming myself happy to be able to contribute to such a work."

The work of Peter Canisius on the Blessed Virgin Mary appeared six years after his work on St. John the Baptist. This delay is explained by the amount of work which a large volume of more than eight hundred pages entails ; but there is a second reason. During this time Peter Canisius was obliged to live in Innsbruck, to preach regularly at first in the church of the Archduke and later in the parish church. In a letter to one of his Superiors he himself explains the delay as follows : " I have not at my disposal a library which is as well stocked as that of Dillingen, and my efforts are absorbed by the duty of preaching. Although we have fifteen Jesuits here, we have much to do by reason of the presence of the Archduke ; furthermore, the air of this town does not

suit me.   I knew all this when I came here ;
but I took no notice because the Father-
General had manifested his will. I shall
continue in the work of my ministry as long
as God gives me strength. I am ready to
die in these mountains, if I am retained by
obedience. Thus I explain my difficulties
in order that you may understand why my
work on the Blessed Virgin has been slow
in appearing."

At Innsbruck, as elsewhere, Peter Canisius
in his sermons had in view only the salvation
of souls. The following anecdote displays
the spirit of faith in his apostolate and shows
that his zeal was not measured by the quality
or the number of his hearers. One day, when
he had to preach, he was not warned that the
Archduke with his Court and the whole town
were present at a tournament. When he
ascended the pulpit, he saw only the small
community of Jesuits and two women. Yet
he preached for a whole hour with such
unction that the Holy Spirit appeared to
speak by his mouth.

Peter Canisius had spent two years in
Innsbruck in his capacity of preacher and
author when he was obliged to go to Rome.
Pope Gregory XIII, who had succeeded

St. Pius V in 1572, was very much concerned
about the state of religion in Central Europe.
" What must be done," he asked Cardinal
Truchsess one day, " to remedy the evils
from which Germany is suffering ? "   " There
is no one who can give you better information than Peter Canisius," replied the Cardinal.
" For thirty years he has worked unceasingly
to cultivate this field which has been filled
with briars.   There is no province, no princi-
pality, which he has not visited and fertilised
by his apostolic labours.   He is beloved of
people and princes, esteemed by the chiefs
of the Church, venerated by all Catholics
and dreaded by Lutherans."   The Sovereign
Pontiff wrote in consequence to Peter
Canisius to consult him on the measures to
be taken for the greater welfare of souls.

He was entrusted with a secret mission
to the Princes of Bavaria and of the Tyrol.
Likewise the Pope expressed a wish to see
him personally.   In the spring of 1573 Peter
Canisius set out for Italy with some of his
brethren, who were going to take part in the
election of a new General of the Society of
Jesus.   About this time Cardinal Otho
Truchsess died in Rome.   His death caused
Peter Canisius great grief, seeing that he

was a protégé of the Cardinal and later his adviser and friend. In the Eternal City Peter Canisius was received kindly by Pope Gregory XIII, with whom he had many long conversations. He impressed the Pope with the necessity of educating good priests for Germany by developing in Rome itself the German College, from which some excellent priests had already come forth, and by founding as many colleges and seminaries as possible in Central Europe. The election of Father Mercurian as General of the Society of Jesus took place without the co-operation of Peter Canisius who was no longer Provincial. However, the Superiors of the Jesuits showed him every respect. Thus, by an exceptional favour, they allowed him to take part in their ordinary meetings. Peter Canisius and some of his brethren were received in special audience by Pope Gregory XIII, who, to facilitate their ministry in Germany and Austria, granted them extended powers which the Jesuits in other countries did not enjoy.

Peter Canisius left Rome very suddenly. He had learned that his name was to appear on the list of ecclesiastics who were to receive the Cardinal's hat, and he withdrew, in order to escape an honour of which he deemed

himself unworthy. It is certain that the
humble Jesuit was not made a Cardinal in
1573 ; but during the Pontificate of Pope
Pius V an incident which occurred in 1568
was related in a letter written to the Emperor
Maximilian by his representative in Rome :
" The nomination of eight Cardinals is discussed. Six names have already been mentioned. Amongst them, especially, is that
of the Jesuit, Canisius. But the latter, it
is said, has heard of the matter, and has
entreated His Holiness to spare him such a
responsibility, which he fears very much.
He asks to remain what he is." Canisius
himself renewed his entreaties with the Pope
and obtained permission to return to Germany
as a simple Jesuit.

On his return to Innsbruck, on the 28th
July, 1573, Peter Canisius resumed his course
of preaching and his work as an author. In
the month of May, 1576, he received a letter
from Rome, by which he was asked to go to
the Diet of Ratisbon to help the Papal
Legate, Cardinal Morone, by his advice.
Peter Canisius remained four months at
Ratisbon, helping the Legate by all means
in his power, also preaching and hearing
confessions in the churches of the town.

Then he departed for Ingolstadt. In 1577 his Superiors observed that he was much exhausted by writing, and dispensed him from issuing new works against the " Centuriators of Magdeburg." Although Peter Canisius was pleased to be released from such responsibility, his efforts were directed to other works. He was at the same time missionary, companion of the Provincial in the visitation of the Houses of the Order, and even Vice-Provincial for a certain time. His brethren and his Superiors willingly consulted him on the most important questions. The holy Jesuit gave his opinions humbly and sincerely, which were not always the same as those of the people who surrounded him.

Peter Canisius was to the Society of Jesus what St. Francis Borgia had desired in 1569. " All the religious of your Province and of the neighbouring Provinces should consider you as their father, as a father to whom the Society in Germany is indebted for all that it has and all that it is." Far from taking advantage of the esteem in which he was held, Peter Canisius remained more faithful than ever to the law of obedience, which he had accepted joyously on his entering into the Society of Jesus : "To follow Jesus Christ, to become like Him, poor, chaste, and obedient in the way of sacrifice ; to give myself entirely to Him . . . to give up my liberty and to put myself in subjection to my Superior, to obey the least sign, and the least command." In these dispositions the holy Jesuit, in 1580, received at Dillingen the command to leave immediately for Fribourg, in Switzerland, in order to found a college there.

CHAPTER IX

ARRIVAL IN SWITZERLAND

FATHER OTTO BRAUNSBERGER, S.J.,[1] thus
describes the arrival of the holy Jesuit :—
" Peter Canisius, born in 1521 at Nymwegen,
in Holland, came in 1580 to Fribourg, in
Switzerland, where he was to pass the last
seventeen years of his life. This is an event
which men did not foresee and which manifested a special design of God. In fact,
some weeks before Canisius set foot on
Swiss soil, neither he nor any of his companions contemplated such a journey. Acting on the advice of Bishop Bonomio, Nuncio
of the Pope in Switzerland, Gregory XIII
had entrusted to the Jesuits of the German
Province the task of opening a college in
Fribourg. Father Hoffaeus, the Provincial,
was to come, accompanied by the Nuncio,
to make arrangements with the people of
Fribourg. But almost on the eve of his
departure he fell ill, and one of the Fathers

[1] *Quatrième Centenaire de la naissance du Bienheureux Pierre
Canisius* Fribourg, 1921, p. 53.

in Munich who had been appointed to replace him was likewise prevented. Then the Provincial had the idea of sending into Switzerland Peter Canisius, who at this time was at Dillingen, quietly occupied in preparing a new edition of his works. Perhaps one might be inclined to see in all this an effect of chance, but later one discovers a well conceived plan of Divine Providence."

One must recall the history of Switzerland at this period. The Swiss had made great efforts to establish centres of higher studies, and soon they called the Society of Jesus to their aid. As early as 1556 they approached Pope Paul III. In was in this year that Peter Canisius was appointed Provincial of the South German Province, and as such was put into communication with Swiss Catholics. In 1560 a request was made to Pope Pius IV, to which the Provincial was invited to give his attention. Assembled at Lucerne in 1565, the deputies of the Catholic Cantons having accepted the Decrees of the Council of Trent, appointed Melchior Lussi to take steps to obtain the co-operation of the Jesuits. It is clear from the letters of Peter Canisius that the Swiss persevered in their intention.

In 1569 Peter Canisius spoke several times
on this subject and mentioned the names of
Rapperswil, Fribourg and Lucerne. In the
same year the new Provincial Father Hoffaeus,
writing to St. Francis Borgia, makes a reference to the possible departure of St. Peter
Canisius for Switzerland. It was eight years
afterwards that the College of Lucerne was
founded, and the turn of Fribourg did not
come until later.

Peter Canisius had been previously interested in the history of Switzerland. In
pursuing his studies in Nymwegen and Cologne
he must surely have heard of those of whom
Pope Julius II spoke as the " Defenders of
the Liberty of the Church." In his prayers
to St. Géréon and the other martyrs of the
Theban legion, whose church was in Cologne,
the thoughts of Peter Canisius were carried
to the mountains of Vallais. The military
virtues of the ancient Swiss were well known
and admired by him. Thus, on the manu-
script of a sermon preached at the Church
of St. Maurice, in Augsburg, and dealing
with the sins to which soldiers are exposed,
he noted in the margin of the text examples
of good soldiers and amongst others the
example of the Swiss, " who must be praised

by reason of their primitive simplicity, their love of liberty, their devotion to religion, and the confidence which they won with princes."

On November 20th, 1580, on the eve of his departure for Switzerland, Peter Canisius wrote to one of his Superiors as follows : " The Provincial sends me to Fribourg to lay the foundation of a college of the Society. . . . To-morrow I shall set out under the protection of Jesus Christ and with your paternal benediction, which I pray for so important a mission. . . . May God's glory be promoted by the task which has been entrusted to me ! " The journey of the holy religious lasted three weeks. He stayed at the Monastery of Paradis, in the Canton Thurgau. In the course of an address to the nuns, by commenting on the name of the convent, he shows how they can make of their abode a really spiritual paradise. At Lucerne Peter Canisius awaited the arrival of Bonomio, the Nuncio, who was to accompany him to Fribourg. He also met there an English Jesuit, Father Andrew, who was to be his fellow-worker. As Peter Canisius did not know French, Father Andrew, who spoke this language, acted as interpreter on the journey.

The two Jesuits and the Nuncio travelled together. While travelling on horseback through the streets of Berne on Saturday morning, the 10th December, at the moment when a criminal was about to be executed, they were recognised as priests and very badly treated. The people insulted them and hurled all kinds of missiles at them. The authorities did nothing, notwithstanding the courageous intervention of a Catholic from Fribourg and of a Deputy from Lucerne. Eventually the Nuncio and his companions succeeded in leaving the unfriendly city. This journey, with its vicissitudes, showed Peter Canisius how much Switzerland resembled the country which he had just left. Thus, as in Germany, religious strife was prevalent. The Canton of Fribourg, which remained faithful to the Catholic religion, with difficulty defended it against the influence of its Protestant neighbours. In Switzerland, then, the Apostle of Ingolstadt, Vienna, and Augsburg, the former Nuncio of the Pope, the author of so many works in defence of religion, was to employ the same weapons and the same remedies. He was to undertake similar toils and undergo similar fatigues.

With these reflections Peter Canisius arrived
in Fribourg. At the sight of the picturesque
city, which is built around its Collegiate
Church, according to his custom he must
surely have prayed and invoked the saints
who protect the city. These saints had long
been familiar to him. He always venerated
St. Nicholas as the highest model of childhood and youth. In the Book of Prayers,
published by him in 1560, a picture, which
has been reproduced several times, represents St. Nicholas and St. Catherine in the
front row of a group of saints which is
dominated by the towering figure of St.
Christopher. The zeal with which St. Peter
Canisius defended the glory of Our Lady
and St. John the Baptist is well known.
St. Maurice was the chief of the Theban
legion. St. Géréon and his companions also
belonged to the same legion, all of whom
St. Peter Canisius had learned to venerate in
Cologne and whose patronage he frequently
invoked in his letters.

The Nuncio and the two Jesuit Fathers
were welcomed with joy and respect by all
who desired the foundation of a College in
Fribourg. On the day after their arrival the
Nuncio and Peter Canisius were officially

received by the Petit Conseil. The scene is described from original documents by F. Ducrest [1] as follows :—

" The Nuncio declares that he has come to greet the governing body and to work with them for the erection of a college, as had already been agreed upon. He brought two Jesuit Fathers, not as many as he desired . . . but not the least, on the contrary the most distinguished in the fear of God and in learning, Peter Canisius, who by his holy life without blemish and by his teaching would certainly do much good amongst them. . . . The Bishop of Vercelli related the regrettable events in Berne. The governing body expressed their surprise and regret which the insult inflicted at Berne caused them. They welcomed the two Fathers and thanked the Nuncio for having brought such a man as Canisius, who was so eminent in learning and in virtue. Three of the principal councillors were entrusted with the duty of taking care of Peter Canisius and of giving him assistance."

The gratitude of the governing body in Fribourg is expressed by a letter which they sent to the Provincial of the Jesuits and

[1] *Quatrième Centenaire de la naissance du Bienheureux Pierre Canisius*; Fribourg, 1921, pp. 135, 136.

8

in which the following words are found [1] :
" We have an excellent reason to rejoice and
to congratulate ourselves on the arrival of
Peter Canisius. We are consoled and com-
pensated amply for the delay of the other
Fathers. We cannot sufficiently thank your
Reverence, who with paternal kindness has
appointed and destined for us such a distinguished man, whose renown has spread
throughout Christendom."

Amongst those who welcomed the coming
of Peter Canisius, in the first place must be
mentioned Peter Schneuwly, Provost and
ordinary preacher of the Collegiate Church
of St. Nicholas. He was a man of great
faith and apostolic zeal. He was an untiring
toiler. He was clever, holy and learned.
He was the source of all the good which was
done in Fribourg during the last forty years
of the sixteenth century. Since 1578 he was
Vicar-General and Administrator of the diocese. At this time the Bishop of Lausanne,
who had been driven from his episcopal see
at the time of the Reformation, had no fixed
abode and generally lived in a foreign country.
Peter Schneuwly had made great efforts, in
conjunction with the Papal Nuncio, to pave

[1] *Saint Pierre Canisius*, by E. Morand ; Fribourg, 1925, pp. 86-7.

the way for the foundation of a college at
Fribourg. Consequently he gave up his
dignity of Provost to devote himself entirely
to preaching. Peter Canisius, who saw him
engaged in this work for more than sixteen
years has praised him in the following terms :
" Who can say how much good he has done
to promote the welfare of the clergy and the
people, how great was his gentleness and the
sweetness of his behaviour, and in how high
regard he was held by the magistrates and
the whole country for his prudence and
firmness ! He had no solicitude for enrich-
ing himself, he who had written so much
and done so much and undertaken so many
works. . . . He had a burning zeal for the
defence of the Catholic religion. He handled
the most difficult business with such extraordinary skill and judgment that he sur-
prised the most accomplished people and
hardly anyone dared to gainsay him. . . .
To sum up in a few words, he replaced the
Bishop with distinction. His preaching was
of great benefit to his fellow-citizens, whom
he confirmed in the Faith. He was a
vigilant prelate, accessible to the people and
the clergy. He was always ready to render
the services which were required of him."

Another member of the Chapter of St.
Nicholas was the parish priest of the town,
Sebastian Werro, who was then only twenty-
five years old. From the earliest days he
was a close friend of Peter Canisius and
became his devoted disciple. He undertook a journey to Rome in 1581 to set before
Pope Gregory XIII several matters concerning the diocese. While passing through
Milan he informed St. Charles Borromeo, and
Bonomio, the Nuncio, concerning the activities of Peter Canisius in Fribourg. From
Rome he set out for Palestine and finally
returned to his own country. His zeal for
the defence of the faith and the reform of
morals occasioned many difficulties. Consequently he gave up his duties as parish
priest and went to Rome to complete his
theological studies. Three years later he
returned to Fribourg with the title of Doctor
and some years later was appointed Provost
and Vicar-General. Sebastian Werro was an
ardent admirer of Peter Canisius and loved
to consult him. After the death of his
venerable friend he did not forget the lessons
in holiness which he had received.

Peter Canisius always had the greatest
regard for his brethren of the Society of

Jesus and also the highest esteem for the members of other religious Orders. Thus, during his stay at Fribourg, he was on intimate terms with the Augustinians and the Conventuals of the Order of St. Francis. One of these Conventuals became the friend of Peter Canisius. His name was Father John Michel, a native of Bulle, and described by Bonomio, the Nuncio, as a man of great worth. At the time when Peter Canisius arrived in Fribourg, this young friar, who was twenty-three years old, already enjoyed the confidence of the Nuncio and the Bishop of the diocese. The Annals of the Monastery of the Conventuals at Fribourg record on January 20th, 1598, the death " of the very pious and learned Father John Michel, Doctor of Theology. He was for many years Vice-Provincial and afterwards Provincial. . . . The province owes much to his extraordinary prudence, justice and meekness. He was appointed Vicar-General by the Bishop of Lausanne (or more precisely, Apostolic Administrator of the Diocese, with Sebastian Werro and Father Licius, Rector of the College of St. Michel), by reason of his numerous great qualities. He laboured with indefatigable zeal for the welfare of his country, and, having rendered the most important service by his remarkable devotion and his sermons in French and German, he died at the early age of forty years." Father Michel made the exercise of St. Ignatius in 1593 under the direction of Peter Canisius. He avowed that he derived more profit from the conferences of the holy and learned Jesuit than from the lectures of his professors of theology in Paris, where he obtained his academical degrees.

CHAPTER X

FOUNDATION OF THE COLLEGE IN FRIBOURG

FROM the beginning the people of Fribourg considered Peter Canisius as one of themselves. In fact he was always devoted to the city and its people. Whenever the question was raised of sending the aged man to a quieter place, as his strength was declining, on each occasion the people of Fribourg set on foot a movement of protest. Thus, for example, in 1584 Sebastian Werro, the parish priest of the city, wrote to the Nuncio, imploring his intervention with the Holy Father, if it were necessary, in the following words[1]: "If this man of God does not return, we shall all perish." He wrote also to St. Charles Borromeo[2]: "God has protected us, and we do not consider the least of his favours to be the gift which he has made to us of Canisius, a model of virtue and prudent simplicity." For his part Peter Canisius did not ask to leave. On the contrary, when his

[1] *Saint Pierre Canisius*, par E. Morand, Fribourg, 1925, p. 95.
[2] Ibid.

brethren, desirous of securing for him a quiet retreat in the centre of his religious province, advised him to take steps discreetly with the people of Fribourg and explain the reasons which rendered his departure suitable, he preferred not to do so and to leave the matter to the decision of his Provincial. The latter thought that it was necessary to leave him in a city where he was venerated almost as a canonized saint, so that it was said : " We have not in our churches the body of a saint ; but we shall have one, if this man of God dies in our midst."

Peter Canisius was favourably impressed, not only by the welcome of the clergy and the people, but also by the appearance of the country. " I am persuaded," he writes, " that there is not in all Catholic Switzerland a place which is better cultivated, more fertile and more favoured from the point of view of the salubrity of the climate and its resources in wine and food than Fribourg, the rival city of Berne, but surpassing all by the cordiality and the inbred politeness of its inhabitants." Werro, the parish priest, a friend of Peter Canisius, says of him that " he found in Fribourg the food and wine which best suited his constitution ; but he made sparing use of them." The principal patron of the city, St. Nicholas, was always specially honoured by him. In the year 1587, when going to Augsburg to attend a meeting of his Order, he was compelled by extreme fatigue, after two days, to return to Fribourg. On this occasion he said : " I see clearly that St. Nicholas does not wish to allow me to leave this city and he is going to oblige me to end my days here."

Peter Canisius had several dwelling places in Fribourg. On his arrival he stayed with his companion in the house of Canon Garin, the Precentor of St. Nicholas—the house which has in our days become the Law Court. It could accommodate at least six religious. The two Jesuits stayed there for nearly two years, saying their Mass in the Church of St. Nicholas, or in the Church of Notre Dame, and taking their meals in the house of Werro, the parish priest, and after some months in the house of Schneuwly, the Provost ; but his Superiors soon decided that Peter Canisius and his companion should take their meals at home, by reason of the danger of dissipation. They said : " the danger, it is true, does not exist in the case of Peter Canisius, who is very venerable, eats very little, and in order not to give bad example would, it seems, allow himself to die of hunger." On the other hand, at that time many people were greatly honoured in receiving Peter Canisius into their houses. Consequently, from time to time he accepted invitations and especially when he saw an opportunity of working for the salvation of souls ; but he always practised the greatest frugality, mixing much water with his wine. His conversation was always serious and breathed of piety. If by chance his companions uttered unbecoming words, he directly reproved them when he judged it necessary, or at least he changed the subject of conversation.

In 1582 the College was founded by Peter Canisius in the Rue de Lausanne, in the house named Ruginet (the seventh in ascending from the hotellerie de l'Autruche), which, subsequently, was called the Maison Gottrau ; this name remains to this day. At first the professors lived in the neighbouring house ; but in the following year they took up their abode in the house called Ruginet. It was here that Peter Canisius lived for thirteen years ; but it is not possible to-day to find any trace of his stay in a house which has several times changed its ownership and undergone many changes. It may be supposed that his room was on the first floor. Father Keller, one of his companions, has related that being at that time a very young Jesuit, he was nevertheless consulted by Peter Canisius, who was working on his Commentaries on the Gospels. One day when Peter Canisius, leaning on his stick, had climbed with great difficulty two floors to see him, Father Keller remarked that he could quite easily have saved him the trouble, seeing that he was so much younger. "A useless old man always has leisure," Peter Canisius answered with a smile, "while a young man should not be taken away from his studies."

The new buildings of the College were situated on the hill of Bisée, or Belsex. In a portion of the ground floor in the north wing, reserved for the Jesuits, Peter Canisius fixed his dwelling during the summer of 1596. It was here that he died in the following year. His room was converted into a chapel in the year 1637. A picture of St. Michael the Archangel is to be seen there, with an inscription dating from 1595, saying that it had adorned the altar of St. Peter Canisius.

It is impossible to enter this room without experiencing a feeling of piety, where there is to be seen an ancient picture of the Saint, on the altar one of his relics, and in an urn the remains of the two coffins which had contained his mortal remains until his beatification, which took place in 1864.

These were the successive dwelling-places of St. Peter Canisius in Fribourg. There are other places in the city or its neighbourhood which recall his presence ; but more especially than these places, the services of every kind which he rendered to the city of his adoption are the reason for speaking quite truly of St. Peter Canisius as a citizen of Fribourg. As a proof, the official record may be quoted by which the Government of Fribourg, on the 12th March, 1626, expressed its homage to the memory of this man, who was so devoted to their country. Among other things we read the following words[1]: " From the moment of his arrival in our midst, the Very Rev. Father Peter Canisius knew admirably how to form and encourage our people in piety, not only by his assiduous and beneficent knowledge, by the teaching of his writings and his practical sermons, but

[1] *Saint Pierre Canisius* ; by E. Morand, Fribourg, 1925, p. 99.

also by the example of a holy life beyond reproach, an example of which the fruit is still visible. He was of modest demeanour and always rendered service to each one promptly, as far as his strength permitted. He often visited the sick, comforted the afflicted, heard the confessions of sinners, and administered the Sacraments with the greatest care. Thus we have testified that our fellow-citizens and subjects, thanks to him, have improved and cultivated virtue with great zeal."

F. Ducrest has said of the foundation of the College of St. Michel : " Schneuwly, the Provost, conceived the project, Bonomio, the Nuncio, gave expression to it, and Father Canisius put it into execution." In order to appreciate the work of St. Peter Canisius it is necessary to relate the course of events before his arrival in Fribourg. F. Ducrest, the historian,[1] writes as follows : " Fribourg had rejected the Reformation owing to the firmness of its rulers, the fidelity of its clergy, and the professions of faith which were made by the inhabitants of the country : but the struggle was long and painful. . . . Surrounded by the powerful

[1] *Quatrième Centenaire de la naissance du Bienheureux Pierre Canisius* ; Fribourg, 1921, p. 121.

Canton of Berne since the conquest of the
Country of Vaud in 1536, the little Canton
of Fribourg was threatened with being overwhelmed by the new doctrines. . . . Faith
was weakened; the spirit of discipline and
the purity of morals in the clergy and people
were subject to many attacks. The Sacraments were little frequented and the churches
were forsaken by the people. All classes of
society suffered more or less. The instruction of the people was neglected. Rich and
influential citizens took more pains in the
training of horses and hunting dogs than
in the education of the young, with a view
to becoming priests, magistrates and enlightened citizens." The young folk destined
for the priesthood, whose means did not
allow them to frequent colleges and universities abroad, were obliged to be instructed
in the primary schools, then in the Latin
school of the town, and, lastly, were initiated
in the work of the ministry under the direction
of parish priests. As for those who went
abroad, they returned with a more extended
knowledge, but sometimes also with indifferent inclinations or a dangerous sympathy
for the new doctrines. This was also the
case with those who were to become the

future magistrates or the powerful laity, who were educated in colleges and universities of the neighbouring Protestant cities.

A higher school was therefore necessary in order to give youth a wider education and especially to give the young folk religious and moral training, also to provide scientific teaching for the benefit of students who were in the habit of going to foreign countries in order to complete their studies.

In 1545 Simon Siebenhart, a German priest, founded a small college, which only lasted ten years. Schneuwly, the Provost, who founded, in 1575, the Chambre des Scolarques—a board of education for the city and adjoining country—opened, in 1577, at the bottom of the Rue des Chanoines, at the entrance to the present bridge of Zähringen, a new school destined to complete the Latin school, which had been reorganised as well as possible some years previously. This new establishment, to which the zealous Provost devoted himself, even teaching in it himself, had great difficulty in continuing to exist, not by reason of want of students —at that time there were three hundred —but because of the poverty of the professors. Schneuwly had heard of the services rendered in different countries by the Colleges of the Society of Jesus, many of which had been founded by Peter Canisius. It was a similar college that he conceived the idea of organising. When Bonomio, the Nuncio, came to Fribourg, the Provost made known to him his project, and the envoy of the Pope hastened to approve of it and to make it his own.

In order to carry out this project, there were two great difficulties to be overcome, namely, the lack of financial resources and the opposition of the Jesuits themselves ; but Bonomio and Schneuwly were men of faith and energy. Bonomio wrote to Schneuwly on September 28th, 1580, as follows [1] :—

" The more obstacles the devil raises, the more necessary it is to be energetic and to advance. The college is part of the designs of Divine Providence. . . . If this college is not established, the religious and moral future of Fribourg is in danger."

The financial problem was solved in the following way. The Nuncio obtained permission from the Sovereign Pontiff to suppress a monastery and to apply its revenues

[1] *Quatrième Centenaire de la naissance du Bienheureux Pierre Canisius* ; Fribourg, 1921, p. 132.

to the proposed college. This monastery was " Sainte Marie d'Humilimont " or " Marsens," which belonged to the Premonstratensians. Having been founded in 1137, it had fallen into decay from the religious and material point of view. The community consisted of only five monks and an abbot. The latter, John Chollet, died on July 1st, 1580, soon after the suppression of his Abbey by the Pope. Of the five remaining monks, three became secular priests and two received an annual pension, which had to be paid by the new College. In addition, the Nuncio had to give an undertaking that the State would not have to make a contribution to the new foundation.

The Jesuits themselves did not give an absolute refusal to come to Fribourg ; but they wished to wait for some years. The reasons they alleged were the following : the lack of professors, and especially of those who knew German and French, the two languages spoken in the Canton of Fribourg ; the great distance between Fribourg and the centre of the South German Province ; the refusal of the State to contribute towards the building of the College ; the inadequate revenue of Marsens ; and, lastly, reluctance

to benefit by the suppression of a religious
house. These objections did not disturb
the Nuncio. He made an advance to the
Society of Jesus and pleaded his cause so
well with the Fathers, and especially the
Provincial, that they considered that they
could not honourably refuse the invitation ;
for this would be to cause grief to such a
virtuous man.   Besides, the Sovereign Pontiff
Pope Gregory XIII himself asked the
Superiors of the Order to send to Fribourg
at least two Jesuits. In this way Peter
Canisius was called upon to found the College.
From its earliest days the foundation of
the College appeared to him to be in the
designs of Divine Providence. He used all
his apostolic zeal to make it a success. He
wrote to one of his friends who was a Jesuit :
" I am at Fribourg as the reaper of an abundant harvest and as the precursor of the college
which is to be founded here. I have no
doubt that from this city, as from a citadel,
Catholics will be able to furnish excellent
weapons to their brethren in Switzerland
and to defend themselves easily against their
formidable adversaries, if only it goes well
with the fortunes of the college."

The first official act of St. Peter Canisius

was to take possession of the Abbey of Humilimont. This was effected on December 21st, 1580, under the Presidency of Bonomio, the Nuncio, and in the presence of witnesses representing the Church and the State, who had come from Fribourg. After the celebration of the Mass of the Holy Ghost, which was sung by the monks, Peter Canisius proclaimed the decision of the Pope, which had the approval of the State, read the Bull, and asked the Nuncio to put him in possession of the suppressed Abbey. The Prelate declared his readiness to execute the Pontifical Document. The bells were rung, Peter Canisius kissed the altar, touched the chalice, and received the keys of the monastery from the Prior. The Nuncio announced to the congregation that the Jesuit Fathers from henceforth were to be the possessors and masters of the house and all its property. The Notary prepared the Document which John de Lanthen-Heid, the Chief Magistrate, confirmed and sealed a few days later. Bonomio left Fribourg a week later, which he was not destined to see again ; but his interest in the religious welfare of the town and especially in the College was unabating. This is clear from the letters which he sent to St. Peter Canisius, for whom he had a great veneration, and of whom he wrote to Schneuwly the Provost[1]: " Take the greatest care in keeping Father Canisius in Fribourg. This venerable old man is a precious jewel, whom you should wrap up in silk."

In giving an undertaking to the Canton not to ask for any assistance in the building of the College, the Nuncio placed the Jesuits, and particularly Peter Canisius, in a difficult position. The revenues of Humilimont were sufficient for the maintenance of the future professors, but not for the construction of the necessary buildings. This difficulty was overcome by the almost miraculous intervention of Peter Canisius. The administration of the property of Humilimont was very complicated. The Jesuits or their agents had to overcome many obstacles, and later they were obliged to sell some of the property of the old monastery. The action of Peter Canisius was to secure the necessary financial aid from the Canton of Fribourg. Such was the ascendancy of the venerable Jesuit over the people and the magistrates that from the outset they could refuse him nothing. Two

[1] *Quatrième Centenaire de la naissance du Bienheureux Pierre Canisius* ; Fribourg, 1921, p. 138.

houses in the Rue de Lausanne were bought, and the classes of the College were commenced on October 18th, 1582. There were soon one hundred and fifty students. A third house was acquired, and in 1584 a new class was added to the three already in existence. Peter Canisius was not appointed Rector. He did not even retain the title of Superior of the small community, and he was no longer a professor. The works of the ministry for the salvation of souls, which he actively pursued, were sufficient to occupy a man of his age, whose great labours had occupied nearly forty years.

On September 11th, 1582, the first Rector, Father Peter Michel, who was of Silesian origin, arrived from Germany. He was accompanied by a brother helper, Michael Sabaudus (Savoy). Upon Father Peter Michel was laid the charge of organising the classes, as well as the great anxiety of the building and administration of the future establishment. Ten days later there came to join him St. Peter Canisius and Father Robert Andrew, four other sons of St. Ignatius, namely, Father John Howlett, who had taught literature and mathematics in Belgium and Germany; Father Stephen

Schönius, Professor for the higher class of Grammar ; Father John Raducius, Professor for the middle class of Grammar ; and Father John Müller, Professor for the lower class of Grammar. Father John Howlett was appointed Prefect of Studies. Father Robert Andrew administered for a time the suppressed monastery of Humilimont, and was the first Procurator of the new college. Thus it is interesting to note that England provided the College of St. Michel with its first Procurator and its first Prefect of Studies.

In addition to rendering the opening of the classes in the College possible, Peter Canisius succeeded in finding a sufficiently large site on which to erect a more suitable building. There was situated on the hill of Bisèe, which overlooked the town, a solid house, a kind of citadel, which had formerly belonged to the Counts of Gruyères and had afterwards become the property of John de Lanthen-Heid, the Chief Magistrate. The latter consented to sell the property to Peter Canisius, together with the garden, the adjoining pond and orchard. Gradually the Jesuits acquired the neighbouring property, and finally possessed all the summit of the hill. On the 13th April, 1584, the Government of the Canton, on the friendly instigation of Gaspard de Baty, Ambassador of the Duke of Savoy, and other friends of the College, determined to build, without any contribution from the Jesuits, at its own expense, the building which was allotted to the classes and the College in which the Fathers afterwards dwelt. The Jesuits undertook to build a large church later. Meanwhile they were content with a temporary chapel. The work was put in hand as soon as possible. Werro, the Provost, testifies that Father Michel, the Rector, laid the foundation stone of the school, and Peter Canisius performed the same ceremony for the other wing of the building.

The work occupied ten years. This was due in the first instance to the bad will of the delegate who was appointed by the Canton to direct it. Later, rumours of war and dangers from Berne were the occasion of urgent fortifications of the city being undertaken. The finances of the Canton were often in a precarious condition. Consequently St. Peter Canisius had to watch closely the periods of activity and stoppage. It is easy to imagine him encouraging the workmen and invoking the blessing of God and the protection of St. Michael upon the work. The great Archangel had been chosen by him as patron of the future church and afterwards of the whole College. Several letters dated from this time express his hopes and anxieties. Sometimes he takes compassion on the workmen commandeered by the State; again he regrets that the Government has asked for help from non-Catholic Cantons. At other times he refers to the objections which were made against the selection of the site. It was said that the children of the town could not, without too much fatigue and serious danger, climb the slopes of the hill to attend the classes, especially in winter, when the roads were covered with snow and ice. The inhabitants, too, who wished to pray in the chapel of the College, would find that it was too far, especially in the early hours of the morning or in the late hours of the evening. There were also surreptitious attacks made by persons who, for religious or political motives, saw a veritable fortress in this building, where foreigners could hide arms and munitions.

Nevertheless, the undertaking of Peter Canisius prospered. The Jesuits made every effort, in Fribourg and elsewhere, to assure the success of the studies. Thus Peter Canisius was occupied in the choice of professors. He endeavoured to procure some from the country itself, and was unsuccessful in persuading Father Etienne Bertin (or Bertigny), the only Jesuit who was a native of Fribourg at that time. The Superiors of the Jesuits secured for the College men of reputation and renown in learning and also noted for their zeal and virtue. During the summer of 1596 the buildings of Bisèe were completed. They were so magnificent that Peter Canisius had some regrets. " It is said," he writes, " that in the whole of France there is no college whose buildings are so spacious and magnificent. Thus we appear to have abandoned humble and holy poverty, which we promised by vow." The opening ceremony took place on the 5th August, of which Canon Werro, an eyewitness, gives the following account [1] : " Father Canisius blessed the building and read the customary prayers. In the classroom, which served as a temporary chapel, he delivered an address, which was the first heard in the College and the last given by

---

[1] *Saint Pierre Canisius*, by E. Morand ; Fribourg, 1925, p. 110.

Canisius. Amongst other things he said that the new house was really built in a place difficult of access and dominating the whole city ; but, he added, ' this is the Lord's doing and it is wonderful in our eyes ' (Psalm cxvii. 23)." The quotation from the Psalms which was made by the holy old man has a remarkable application to the foundation of the College, a work which was really amazing, and humanly speaking almost impossible, but which was brought about by God in making use of men as His providential instruments, at the head of whom was Peter Canisius.

CHAPTER XI

APOSTLE OF FRIBOURG

THE last seventeen years of the life of St. Peter Canisius were occupied in the foundation and progress of the College of St. Michel and also in the active works of the ministry for the salvation of souls. For eight and a half years, that is to say, from the end of 1580 until the spring of 1589, one of the principal occupations of Peter Canisius was preaching.

From Easter, 1589, he seldom preached, but continued his instructions by his writings. It was at this time that most of his works, which were published in Fribourg, appeared. Peter Canisius wrote, himself, or dictated his instructions to a Jesuit, at least in the form of a detailed synopsis. It is thus that most of his sermons have been preserved; three hundred and twenty sermons were preached in Fribourg. Soon after his arrival in Fribourg it was decided that St. Peter Canisius should preach in German at the Collegiate Church of St. Nicholas on feast days and Sundays, which duty had previously been performed by Schneuwly, the Provost.

On December 18th, 1580, when St. Peter Canisius for the first time ascended the pulpit of the Church of St. Nicholas, his hearers were aware of his great reputation as an orator, and many had read his celebrated catechism, which, since 1577, had been used in the schools of the Canton of Fribourg. The Annals of the College thus describe the effect of his preaching in 1583 : " His sermons were well attended, especially in Lent, when the subject was the Holy Sacrifice of the Mass. The public processions are better attended, and there is progress in the observance of fasting. Likewise there is an increase in the number of Communions ; six hundred persons received Holy Communion at Christmas, whereas formerly there were only five or six communicants. Two thousand Confessions were heard in Holy Week . . . fifty-six heretics have returned to the Catholic Church, and several of them belong to important Swiss families. Besides the Government has made several useful decisions, for example, that Holy Viaticum should be brought to the sick with more

honour. . . . Our missionaries, who have gone
to country parishes where there were several
abuses, have caused a remarkable advance
in morality. The parish priests themselves
have learned to fulfil their duties better
towards their flocks. . . . Explanations of
the Catechism in three churches of the town
have been attended, not only with the
greatest advantage to young people, but
they have also been heard with pleasure
by priests and the influential laity."

The explanation of the Catechism completed the teaching of St. Peter Canisius.
It was entrusted to the Jesuits in 1583.
The instructions were given in German in
the Church of Notre Dame and in the Church
of St. John ; but they were given in French
in the Chapel of St. Peter in the Upper
Town. The Government instituted many
reforms on the advice of Peter Canisius.
Thus, in 1584, it was decreed that a solemn
profession of the Catholic Faith should be
made in the whole Canton of Fribourg. A
similar profession of faith had not been made
since 1561.

The reform in morals proceeded slowly.
He indicated as being grave some sins
which were considered to be venial, namely,

hardness towards the poor, abandonment of
Divine Worship, impurity, neglect of the
duties of one's state in life, and especially
drunkenness. The Bishops of Switzerland,
in their letter dated May 1st, 1921, lay stress
upon the moral reforms effected by St. Peter
Canisius in the following passage : " It is
important to draw attention to the fact that
Peter Canisius used all means to bring about
a real reformation in the countries to which
God had sent him. His first care was to
improve morality by suppressing disorders
which were then prevalent. While he recalled dignitaries to a sense of their duties
in general, on whom responsibility princip-
ally rested, he did not refrain from dwelling
upon the smallest details. For example, in
Fribourg he raised his voice against the bad
attendance at religious services, the arbitrary
rise in the price of provisions, and injustice
towards servants. He did not fear to appeal
to the laws and even to exert very strong
pressure on the magistrates to redress mis-
conduct. With holy liberty and only having
in view obedience to the law of God, he
pursued abuses in every place where he
encountered them, endeavouring to abolish
them by practical and effective measures

rather than condemning them by rhetorical effusions."

St. Peter Canisius founded two Confraternities of Our Lady. The first, consisting of men, was established on September 8th, 1581, in the Church of Notre Dame, which included clergy, magistrates, and other laymen. On November 1st, in the same year, he instituted the Confraternity for students, which met at first in the Church of Notre Dame and afterwards in the temporary College Chapel in the Rue de Lausanne. The first Prefect was Pancratius Python, who had addressed Peter Canisius in Latin at the time of his arrival in Fribourg and was the first to serve his Mass. Furthermore, about this time the Women's Confraternity was instituted. Its foundation was probably due to the efforts of St. Peter Canisius; and its statutes were composed by Sebastian Werro, the parish priest, under the inspiration and perhaps at the dictation of his holy friend.

The city of Fribourg was not the only place to benefit by the teaching of St. Peter Canisius. He preached in the country parishes where German was spoken, and visited others where the language was French.

The following places were visited by him
and his companions : Gruyères, Bulle, Esta-
vayer, Attalens, Echarlens, Châtel-St.-Denis,
and Farvagny. Sometimes he undertook
more distant journeys. On January 7th,
1581, he set out for Lucerne in the company
of the deputies from Fribourg, who were
going to take part in a meeting of the
Catholic Cantons. Some time afterwards he
went to Soleure to support Bonomio the
Nuncio. In 1584 he was at Augsburg, attending a meeting of the Jesuits of the South
German Province. Later he visited Lucerne
again, where he preached to large numbers of
people, and on this journey he exercised his
ministry in Baden, which is situated in the
Canton of Aargau. In the same year St.
Peter Canisius went on a pilgrimage to
Einsiedeln and took part on September 14th
in the Feast of the Dedication of the Church.
In 1587 St. Peter Canisius was summoned to
another meeting of his Order ; but on this
occasion, as already related, he had to turn
back when he reached Baden and return to
Fribourg, where St. Nicholas willed that he
was from henceforth to remain. Now his
strength gradually diminished and soon he
was compelled to give up preaching, that is

to say, one of the most important works of his life.

In view of the Encyclical Letter (*Casti Connubii*) of Pope Pius XI *On Christian Marriage*, dated 31st December, 1930, it is interesting to recall a passage of a sermon preached by St. Peter Canisius at Innsbruck. On the subject of vocations, he thus speaks pertinently to his hearers[1] : " Not only does vocation to the clerical or religious state come from God, but also vocation to marriage and the family life. The main point is to understand well the duties of one's vocation and to remain faithful to them. It may happen that a person whose state of life in itself is less holy may be more pleasing to God than another person whose vocation is more perfect."

Peter Canisius is less known to us as a preacher than as a writer, because nearly all his sermons have not yet been published. The sermons which he preached at Augsburg (1559-1566) are reckoned in hundreds, and the manuscripts are preserved. Father Otto Braunsberger, S.J.,[2] says that " he dictated them for the most part and preferably in Latin ; but they were all delivered in German.

[1] *Quatrième Centenaire de la naissance du Bienheureux Pierre Canisius;* Fribourg, 1921, pp. 109, 110.   [2] Ibid.

10

One observes that he has reviewed and corrected with his own hand extracts written by his secretary. Statements, divisions, proofs, replies to objections, and practical conclusions are all arranged with the most scrupulous care. One of his colleagues relates that sometimes he passed a large part of the night in preparing his sermon for the next day."

Whatever were the subjects of his instructions, Peter Canisius used all the resources of his knowledge and piety. In the first place, he had a profound knowledge of Sacred Scripture. At Cologne, as a student, he read a part of it every day ; he began his career as a teacher by expounding it, and he never ceased afterwards to study and meditate upon it. He said that " The best use that man could make of his eyes is to shed tears of love for God and to read Holy Scripture." Consequently, in his letters and other writings, and, with much more reason, in his sermons, the words, comparisons and examples of the Bible come naturally to his mind. In the text of Scripture he did not consider exclusively the literal sense, but, as he says himself : " He endeavours to draw from it practical teaching which attentive reading manifests. Thus he satisfies, if not the learned, at least simple readers of good-will, whose minds must not only be enlightened but their hearts also stirred to piety."

In the second place, Peter Canisius was well versed in the writings of the Fathers of the Church. He quoted them with the same ease as the Bible ; for he had an excellent memory. His first biographer, Father Matthew Raderius, S.J., in 1614, furnishes a proof by mentioning the following incident : " During the first month after his arrival in Fribourg, Father Canisius received hospitality from Sebastian Werro (parish priest of the Collegiate Church of St. Nicholas). One day the latter spoke to him about a passage from St. Basil, the exact words of which he had not succeeded in finding. Immediately Canisius, without hesitation, not only indicated the book but even the chapter which contained the words in question."

In the third place, Peter Canisius did not entirely exclude the testimony of non-Catholic writers in the defence of Catholic truth. Thus, in his explanation of the Gospel for Easter Monday, he makes the following observation : " Although I must above all give my full and entire faith to what Holy

Writ says of Christ Who is God and the Son of Mary, I shall readily admit the witness of those who, being strangers to the true faith, yet agree on certain points with Holy Scripture and thereby confirm Christian truth. Thus, after the Sibylline books, I shall make use of Josephus, a Jew esteemed by Roman writers as well as by our ancient theologians."

The activity of St. Peter Canisius as a preacher may be gauged from the fact that the manuscripts of about two thousand sermons concerning faith and morals delivered by him fill thirty-three volumes, as is specially indicated in the Decretal Letter [1] of Pope Pius XI, which was issued on the occasion of his canonization, May 21st, the Feast of the Ascension, 1925.

---

[1] *Acta Apostolicae Sedis,* 1925, vol. xvii, p. 353.

CHAPTER XII

APOSTOLATE EXERCISED BY WRITING

St. Peter Canisius, at an early age, understood the importance of the circulation of good books in the formation of a holy and learned clergy worthy of their vocation, and in fostering faith and piety among the faithful. " The whole life of Canisius," writes the Protestant theologian, Gautier,[1] " is animated by the desire to form a generation of devout clerics capable of serving the Church worthily." While he was still a theological student in Cologne and a novice of the Society of Jesus, he commenced the apostolate of the written word by editing the works of ecclesiastical authors. The first result of his labours was a German edition of the sermons and other writings of John Tauler, the Dominican, a great mystic of the fourteenth century, whose activity was witnessed on the banks of the Rhine from Basle to Cologne. This work appeared in 1543, soon after his admission into the Society of Jesus. It is not only

[1] *Étude sur la correspondance de Pierre Canisius;* Geneva, 1905, p. 46.

the first book of St. Peter Canisius but also
the first literary effort published by a Jesuit.
St. Peter Canisius is thus at the head of the
host of distinguished writers belonging to the
Society of Jesus.

In the following years the young Jesuit
prepared a new edition of the works of two
great Bishops and Doctors of the Church,
who flourished in the fifth century, and whose
writings appeared to him especially useful
in proving the truth of the Catholic faith
against the errors of the Lutherans. In
1546, after his ordination to the priesthood,
he edited in Latin the works of St. Cyril of
Alexandria, in three folio volumes; and
afterwards, in the same year, there appeared
the sermons and letters of St. Leo the Great,
combined in one volume, preceded by a
biographical sketch written by our Saint.

It is difficult to see how St. Peter Canisius
contrived to find the time to write all he did.
He was Provincial of the South German
Province for thirteen years—an office which
provides more than enough work for an
ordinary man—and, in this capacity, made
frequent journeys. His duties as preacher
at the Cathedral at Augsburg occupied much
of his time. He spent many months at

court or parliament on diplomatic missions; and yet in the midst of it all he was always preparing something useful for the Press. In 1562 St. Peter Canisius brought out an edition of the Letters of St. Jerome for school use. This work met with great success and was reprinted no less than forty times in different countries.

Whenever there was need of literature of any kind, he was ready. Melancthon, in his Latin Grammar, mingled the errors of Protestantism with the rules of grammar. Consequently, Peter Canisius wrote, in 1556, a Latin Grammar, an adaptation of Father Hannibal Codret's, in which the same device was used. There is an appendix containing some prayers and a compendium in Latin of the Catholic religion, to serve the purposes of translation. This compendium or summary was the first edition of the small Catechism, consisting of fifty-nine questions and answers in Latin, divided into six chapters corresponding to those of the large Catechism —the fifth chapter here being divided into two parts. In the same year this summary appeared in German with the following title: "Small Catechism with some Prayers for the Use of Simple Folk."

Peter Canisius understood the educational value of pictures. Thus he used the art of illustration in his Catechism. In 1589, Christopher Plantin, at the request of Peter Canisius, published the pictorial Catechism, consisting of one hundred and seven copper engravings by Peter van den Borcht, with extracts from the middle-sized or intermediate Catechism.

The letters of Peter Canisius fill nine volumes, the first eight of which contain on an average one thousand pages each. Father Otto Braunsberger, S.J., in his admiration for the extraordinary and varied activity of Peter Canisius, says [1] that "Canisius preaches so much that one would say he was accustomed only to preach ; while seeing he writes so much, one would think that he had no other occupation ; he has such frequent communications with Popes, Nuncios, Bishops or Princes, that one cannot conceive how he could find time for other works."

While residing in Cologne, at the age of twenty-four, he was chosen by the clergy and university to appeal to the Emperor Charles V concerning Hermann von Weid, the Archbishop, who was planning with

[1] *Quatrième Centenaire de la naissance du Bienheureux Pierre Canisius ;* Fribourg, 1921, p. 107.

Melancthon to introduce Protestant writings into his diocese. His suit was successful, and the sentence of deposition, passed by Pope Paul III against Hermann von Weid, was carried into effect.

The work of St. Peter Canisius in promoting the apostolate of the Catholic Press is described by Father Otto Braunsberger, S.J., in the following passage[4]:—"Canisius held that to defend the Catholic truth with the pen was just as important as to convert the Hindus. At Rome and Trent he strongly urged the appointment at the Council, at the Papal Court, and in other parts of Italy, of able theologians to write in defence of the Catholic faith. He begged Pius V to send yearly subsidies to the Catholic printers of Germany, and to permit German scholars to edit Roman manuscripts; he induced the City Council of Fribourg to erect a printing establishment, and he secured special privileges for printers. He also kept in touch with the chief Catholic printers of his time—Plantin of Antwerp, Cholin of Cologne, and Mayer of Dillingen—and had foreign works of importance reprinted in Germany, for example, the works of Andrada,

[1] *Catholic Encyclopaedia*, vol. xi. p. 759.

Fontidonio, and Villalpando, in defence of the Council of Trent.

"Canisius advised the Generals of the Order to create a college of authors ; urged scholars like Bartholomaeus Latomus, Friedrich Staphylus, and Hieronymus Torrensis to publish their works ; assisted Onofrio Panvinio and the polemic, Stanislaus Hosius, by reading their manuscripts and correcting proofs ; and contributed to the work of his friends, Surius, on the Councils. At his solicitation the *Briefe aus Indien*, the first relations of Catholic missioners, were published (Dillingen, 1563-1571)."

"Canisius," wrote the Protestant preacher, Witz,[1] "by this activity gave an impulse which deserves our undivided recognition, indeed which arouses our admiration." The ministry of teaching by writing, which Peter Canisius had begun even before his ordination to the priesthood, he continued almost to the moment of his death. In fact, a month before his death, he published a new edition of his *Manuel des Catholiques*, and on the day before his death he dictated a letter to his brother, Theodoric, who was a Jesuit, like himself.

---

[1] *Petrus Canisius;* Vienna, 1897, p. 12.

An ancient biographer says that Peter Canisius always made himself useful to those who were absent by his letters, which always, without exception, breathed the odour of antiquity and holiness, which is characteristic of the early Fathers. This is all the more true of the last years of our Saint. From his cell in Fribourg letters were issued to people of all ages and classes. Very frequently they were replies to questions on subjects of all kinds. Among the correspondents of St. Peter Canisius at this period of his life are to be found St. Charles Borromeo, St. Francis de Sales, several Cardinals and Bishops, a future Emperor, German Princes, ecclesiastics and lay people, in Switzerland and in other countries, and, lastly, the General of the Jesuits, Father Aquaviva, who had an almost filial regard for the Founder of the College of St. Michel in Fribourg,[1] "who," he said, "has deserved well of the Order for so many years by his writing and activity, and on whose prayers and advice I rely to work with advantage for the glory and honour of God."

St. Charles Borromeo, the illustrious Archbishop of Milan, and one of the most

[1] *Saint Pierre Canisius*, by E. Morand; Fribourg, 1925, p. 127.

remarkable benefactors of Switzerland, wrote
three times to St. Peter Canisius. He asked
his Superiors, in vain, to have him as a companion and counsellor during his apostolic
visit to Switzerland. Failing the company
of the holy Jesuit, he received from him
valuable information on several points which
he had submitted to him, especially with
regard to Fribourg, and particularly concerning the place where the Bishop of
Lausanne should reside.

St. Francis de Sales was still Provost of
the Chapter of Geneva. For nine months
he had been evangelising the Chablais and
had only gathered part of the great harvest
of souls when he wrote to St. Peter Canisius
a letter, expressing the wish to be in contact
with him and desiring to have recourse to
his learning for the interpretation of a passage
in the Book of Genesis. No one has given
greater praise to St. Peter Canisius than the
future Bishop of Geneva. The reply of St.
Peter Canisius to St. Francis de Sales has
not yet been traced.

The books which St. Peter Canisius published are of great value to Catholics. During
the last years of his life, when he was unable
to preach, his literary activity was very

great. It is worthy of note that on his arrival in Fribourg his first care was to set up a printing press. Long experience had taught him the necessity of the press, in the fullest meaning of the word, for the development of theological and other sciences, and for the defence of the Church. In one of his first letters, written after his arrival in Switzerland, addressed to Bonomio the Nuncio, he expressed the wish that one of the Frobenius, who were printers in Basle, should be established in Fribourg. This project was not realised. It was only in 1585 that Abraham Gemperlin, a printer from Freibourg in Breisgau, came to the city. The Government wrote to Pope Sixtus V to obtain the customary authorisation and privileges for this publisher. In this letter the following words are found[1] : "On the recommendation of the Rev. Father Peter Canisius, Theologian of the Society of Jesus, who greatly honours our city by his presence, we have, not without little expense, acquired a printing press and engaged a printer."

Werro, the Provost, writes as follows[2] :— "When Switzerland had become the scene of the activity of Peter Canisius, he did not

[1] *Saint Pierre Canisius*, by E. Morand ; Fribourg, 1925, pp. 130, 131. [2] Ibid.

desire that the works of his later years should be confined to one city. He wished his activity to extend by his writings to all the churches of the country. He wrote *The Life of St. Beatus* for the people of Lucerne and the inhabitants of Aargau ; *The Life of St. Ursus the Martyr*, for the people of Soleure ; *The Life of St. Fridolin*, for Glaris and the country of Seckingen, and, lastly, he wrote *The Story of St. Maurice and His Companions*, for the people of Vallais. In addition he composed a prayer-book, *Manuel des Catholiques*, for the use of all the faithful."

To this list must be added *The Life of St. Ida of Toggenbourg*, *The Life of St. Meinrad*, and a book entitled *Méditations et Prières du Frère Klaus d'Unterwalden*, which manifests the veneration of St. Peter Canisius for Blessed Nicholas of Flüe. For this reason the Apostle of Fribourg may be truly called the Apostle of Switzerland. Father Otto Braunsberger, S.J., says[1] : " These biographies of popular saints, which are full of texts of Holy Scripture and quotations from the Fathers, prove to the Swiss that their faith is, indeed, the heritage of the primitive

---

[1] *Quatrième Centenaire de la naissance du Bienheureux Pierre Canisius;* Fribourg, 1921, p. 61.

church, and that it has been confirmed by numerous remarkable miracles."

The two most important books written by St. Peter Canisius during his stay in Fribourg are written in Latin and are entitled *Notae in evangelicas lectiones* (Notes on the Gospel Readings). The first volume contains about twelve hundred pages and appeared in 1591. It explains the gospels of the Sundays and may be used as a prayer-book and a meditation book. It is dedicated to Peter Schneuwly, the Vicar-General ; Ehrard Thorin, the Provost, and to the clergy of Fribourg. The author says : " I thought it my duty to perform by writing what I am unable to do by speaking on account of my age, and also to give evidence of my ardent desire to work amongst you for the salvation of souls." The second volume, dedicated to the Government of Fribourg, deals with the Gospels for Feast days. It is dated 1593, and is introduced by Latin verse composed by William Techtermann, the Chancellor, a poet of distinction. The coming of Peter Canisius to Fribourg is recorded by him as a remarkable favour of God in the following words : " The King of ages, fulfilling our wishes, grants us help so much desired, by

sending into our midst men renowned for
their faith and piety . . . at their head
Canisius shines by his merits, his venerable
age, and the remarkable works which he has
published." The second volume also contains a short letter, by which Monsignor
Antoine de Gorrevod, Bishop of Lausanne,
gives his approval to the two volumes and
makes their use obligatory for the secular and
regular clergy, at the same time imposing
upon them the duty of making these books
known.

In his explanation of the Gospels St. Peter
Canisius followed the calendar of the Diocese
of Lausanne. There is a brief commentary
on each Gospel, of which the text is given ;
then follow meditations on the more important verses ; lastly, the author recom-
mends certain intentions for prayer.

CHAPTER XIII

LAST YEARS AND DEATH OF ST. PETER CANISIUS

CONTEMPORARY writers make only a few references to the pilgrimages of St. Peter Canisius to Bourguillon. But the ancient tradition, which represents him climbing the steep slope leading to the ancient sanctuary, is mentioned by his later biographers. He preached there several times. He sent or led pilgrims to the Shrine of Our Lady. There he obtained the favour of a cure for one of his companions. It was at his instigation that the members of the confraternities founded by him established a custom of making regular pilgrimages to this Shrine.

St. Peter Canisius, owing to his infirmities, caused by his austerities, was compelled to give up preaching in churches from the year 1589. Henceforth, from time to time, he preached to his brethren, for example, on the occasion of the renewal of their annual vows. In 1591 he had a stroke of paralysis, and came very near to death. The Blessed Sacrament was exposed in all the churches of Fribourg, and the people went in pilgrimage to the various shrines in the district to pray for his recovery. He got sufficiently well again to renew his studies and his writings, with which he associated Father Ilsung as his secretary. Henceforward he had to help himself along with a stick. In his letters of this period he complains, not of his sufferings, which he considers to be a favour of Divine Providence, but rather of his illness, which makes him an unprofitable servant, who is content to live without rendering service and who is restricted to supporting each day the pains and infirmities of old age. He asks humbly for the prayers of those who surround him, and his intentions at different times are mentioned amongst those which were proposed at this period by the confraternities which he had inaugurated.

In 1596, in a letter written to Father Aquaviva, his Superior-General, he said : " Being exempted from the duties of our Order, I have commenced taking my meals in my room and saying Mass in the private oratory. I no longer render any services to our brethren or to strangers. Thus I become lazy, idle and useless, like a barren tree which forebodes ruin. I am not worth the bread which I eat, nor the attention of my brethren, which their charity lavishes upon an ungrateful man. I am troubled, seeing that I do not take sufficient advantage of this kind attention to be better prepared for the great journey and to be enabled to answer the call of Our Lord."

This was the great preoccupation of Peter Canisius, especially during the last year of his life. Divine Providence favoured him in many ways. Thus, for example, by a miracle God provided him one day with an uncommon bird, the only food which he could then take. God also detached him from this world by removing his best friends by death. In the autumn of 1596 Father Michel, his Superior, died ; soon afterwards his doctor, Peter Kuntzli, a very learned and pious man, was carried off by the plague. The same epidemic in the following year caused the death of Schneuwly, the Provost, who was a victim of his devotion to the plague stricken. In the beginning of September, 1597, St. Peter Canisius was struck in his turn. In addition to his habitual infirmities were added dropsy, congestion of the lungs, and ulcers in the throat. From this day he

had to give up saying Mass, and he could no
longer leave his room. His bed was even
painful to him. He remained seated part of
the day, being troubled because he could do
nothing, "which was not true," as Werro
remarks,[1] "for passing over his acts of
patience, he gave himself up to meditation
in the morning, and in the evenings he recited
long prayers, which were a substitute for
the Divine Office, since his Breviary had
been taken away from him. He had great
consolation in considering the benefits of
God, Who had foreseen the way in which his
life should end, and Who had given him the
grace not to leave this world without
suffering."

There is a story related concerning the
patience with which St. Peter Canisius endured his last illness. Sebastian Strang came
to the College at Fribourg in the spring of
1597. He was Sacristan and Infirmarian.
He lived with St. Peter Canisius for nine
months. Having heard of the fame of his
sanctity, he determined to put his virtue
to the test. One day the old man had asked
him to light his stove before the usual time.
The young Jesuit pretended to obey. With

[1] *Saint Pierre Canisius*, by E. Morand ; Fribourg, 1925, p. 144.

much ado he arranged the wood, which he did not light. After a short time St. Peter Canisius, who had waited in vain for warmth, was not only not disturbed ; but blessing God and thanking the brother, he went quietly to bed. Another day the same brother refused openly to gratify the desire of the sick man. The latter replied with such gentleness that the infirmarian went away in confusion, repenting of his action. One month before his death, when the infirmarian was otherwise engaged, S^t. Peter Canisius was so weak that he fell from his chair, and being unable to get up unaided, he remained for a long time on the ground without calling for help. On the return of the brother he showed no resentment ; but on the contrary he said that this accident would not prevent them from remaining good friends.

One day Sebastian Strang was reading aloud *The Lives of the Saints*, by Surius, and thought within himself that he was wrong by so doing and in not continuing his studies. Peter Canisius, by revelation, was aware of his thoughts ; for he suddenly interrupted the reader in the following words : " My brother, put away this thought and let us remain in humility." When the brother, in confusion, attempted to deny his thoughts, St. Peter Canisius replied : " Yes, indeed, you have had this thought. As for me, if I obtained permission from my Superiors, I should have been delighted to undertake this duty of assisting a brother." Sebastian Strang, in the narrative of this event, says : " Full of respect I threw myself at his feet, asking his pardon, and I did so because he was so soon going to enjoy the presence of God. I entreated him to obtain for me the grace of perseverance and sincere humility. He promised to do so. Then I asked for his blessing. Smiling kindly, he granted my request and uttered the blessing, stretching his hands over my head while I was bathed in tears."

In the midst of his sufferings he continued his exercises of piety and dictated his letters. The last letter, addressed to his brother, Theodoric, and dated December 20th, 1597, unfortunately has been lost. On December 17th he was visited by two Capuchins, Father Anthony de Canobbio, Guardian of the Monastery of Lucerne, and Brother Leander Renaud, a novice, who came from Romont. The latter had returned to his native town to regulate the affairs of his family with

the assistance of his Superior. On the
advice of Peter Canisius he gave his property to the Church of Romont in order to
enhance the glory of the divine worship.

The holy old man felt that the moment
of his death was near, and in consequence
he asked to have the Last Sacraments administered to him. On December 20th,
Father Licius, Rector of the College of St.
Michel, noticed that Peter Canisius was
rapidly sinking, and warned him to prepare
his soul to leave this world. Consequently,
Peter Canisius confessed his sins, and in
accordance with his request the seven peni-
tential psalms were recited on his behalf,
from which he drew great consolation. St.
Peter Canisius told his infirmarian to go to
bed, because, he said, he would not die that
night. The infirmarian obeyed : but full of
anxiety he returned about midnight to ask
if he desired to receive Holy Communion.
The holy old man told him to continue his
rest as he could wait until the morning.

On the following day, which was Sunday,
he received Holy Viaticum about five o'clock.
About eleven o'clock Sebastian Werro, the
Provost, relates that he began to say the
Rosary. At this moment it is said that he

was strengthened by an apparition of Our Lady, whom he contemplated with eyes shining with joy, at the same time continuing his pious colloquies. In the afternoon he received the Sacrament of Extreme Unction. A short time afterwards, in the presence of the Fathers of the college, the two Capuchins just mentioned, namely, Father Anthony de Canobbio and Brother Leander Renaud, Christopher Reyff, a Councillor, and Anthony de Montenach, the Chancellor, he gave up his soul to God, in peace, at a quarter to four in the afternoon of December 21st, in the year 1597, in the seventy-eighth year of his age, having lived seventeen years in Fribourg. At the moment of his death, Nicholas Wild, a Councillor, saw a globe of fire over the room in which St. Peter Canisius died, which he pointed out to his daughter Elizabeth.

The funeral took place in the Church of St. Nicholas, and on his tomb, in front of the high altar, were engraved the following words : " This is a memorial to our venerable Father Peter Canisius, Theologian of the Society of Jesus. This monument was erected in 1597 by the nobles Nicholas, Roch, George and Peter, brothers belonging to the Diesbach family."

Father Matthew Raderius, S.J., in his *Life of St. Peter Canisius*, written in 1614, gives the following brief sketch of his brother Theodoric, who was also a Jesuit, and which affords an illustration of the spirit of prophecy possessed by the Saint.

Born at Nymwegen in 1532, Theodoric Canisius was very successful in his studies and obtained the degree of Master of Arts. Being aware of his vocation to be a religious, and acting on the advice of his elder brother, he set out for Rome in 1554. He was admitted into the Society of Jesus and was honoured with the special confidence of St. Ignatius. Some years later he was sent to Germany, where with success he directed colleges at Munich, Dillingen and Ingolstadt. For a time he took his brother's place as Provincial. Afterwards he was stationed at the Jesuit College in Lucerne and became Rector of the University in Ingolstadt. Then he returned to Lucerne. In 1597 he was given permission to travel to Fribourg to visit Peter Canisius, who was dangerously ill. At this time Peter Canisius uttered a saying which impressed him and which he related to his brethren on his return to Lucerne. It was : " When you hear of my

death, Theodoric, something serious will
happen to you." A little while afterwards
a letter from Fribourg announced the death
of Peter Canisius ; at these tidings, Theodoric
was struck with apoplexy. Paralysed and
deprived of the use of speech, with the
exception of invoking the names of Jesus
and Mary, he lived for seven years and died
at Ingolstadt in 1604. The prediction made
to Father Theodoric was quoted in the
process of beatification as a proof of the
spirit of prophecy possessed by the illustrious
servant of God.

CHAPTER XIV

BEATIFICATION AND CANONIZATION OF ST. PETER CANISIUS

AFTER the death of St. Peter Canisius the Jesuits commenced to build a church. This was accomplished from their own resources and the gifts which were given to them in the Canton of Fribourg and outside its borders. This church was dedicated to St. Michael, and was commenced in 1604. It was opened for Divine Worship in 1610 and consecrated in 1613 by Monsignor de Watteville, Bishop of Lausanne. The church was completed in 1623. It was quite natural that the Jesuits wished to have the remains of St. Peter Canisius in their midst. It was only in 1625, after long negotiations, that the Chapter of St. Nicholas and the Government consented to the translation of his precious relics. They were carried in solemn procession through the town to the church of the college, where they were buried in the middle of the choir. The faithful flocked to

this new tomb ; yet many still went to the
Church of St. Nicholas to pay homage to St.
Peter Canisius at his first resting place, before
his picture, and at the foot of the pulpit where
he had so often expounded the Word of God.

God rewarded this persevering piety by
spiritual and temporal favours. St. Peter
Canisius, in his lifetime, had already enjoyed
the power of working miracles and the gift
of prophecy. Thus, William Krummenstoll,
a councillor and an old man, who, on his
return from Hauterive to Fribourg, had
fallen with his horse into a moat and, not
being able to extricate himself, was about
to be overwhelmed, was suddenly delivered
by invoking the help of God through the
merits of St. Peter Canisius. He had narrated
this accident to no one ; and yet his venerable
friend recalled to him the exact details,
adding these words : " Thank God and do
not speak of me." Shortly before his death
St. Peter Canisius promised Werro, the
Provost, to intercede with God for the
preservation of the people from pestilence.
From that day the town, which had often
been afflicted by this scourge, was left
unscathed for many years.

After his death the power of the intercession of St. Peter Canisius was especially manifested. His body having been taken in a solemn procession from the Chapel of the College of St. Michel to the Collegiate Church of St. Nicholas, the people crowded around the open coffin to get a last glimpse of him, whom all regarded as a father. In the throng was a pious woman of Fribourg, who had long since been suffering from an incurable disease, namely, epilepsy. She had come into the church, pondering within herself, as the woman in the Gospel, with great confidence, the words : " If I shall touch only his garment, I shall be healed " (Matt. ix. 21). However, she was prevented by the multitude from drawing nigh to the remains of the servant of God. Consequently, unknown to all, she hid herself in the church, and remained the whole night in prayer near his sacred body, which had already been placed in the tomb. Her devotion was not in vain ; for at daybreak she returned to her home completely cured, and as long as she lived she was free from that disease.[1]

In 1740 it was noted that more than two hundred favours, some of which were cures

[1] This miracle is related in the Decretal Letter of Pope Pius XI, to which reference has been made at the end of Chapter XI. *Acta Apostolicae Sedis*, 1925, vol. xvii. p. 356.

from disease, had been obtained from God, in Fribourg and elsewhere, in answer to the prayers offered at the tomb of St. Peter Canisius, before one of his pictures, or by the application of objects which had belonged to him. Among these objects may be mentioned, letters which he had written with his own hand, his rosary, his biretta, pieces of his clothing, and the shroud used for the translation of his body in 1625. The remains of St. Peter Canisius rested in the tomb before the high altar in the Church of St. Michel until the end of the process of beatification. In 1697 the first centenary of the death of the servant of God was solemnly celebrated. The faithful were warned that there was no question of cult given to Peter Canisius but of thanksgiving to God, who through his instrumentality had preserved the faith in Fribourg.

From 1625 to 1690 the ecclesiastical investigations of his virtues and miracles were conducted by the Bishops of Lausanne, Dillingen, and Freising. Then the disturbances of wars prevented further progress in the cause of his beatification. The apostolic proceedings began in 1734, in accordance with the instructions issued by Pope Clement

XII at the request of numerous Bishops, the Emperor, and many Princes. In 1741 the remains were identified; but the proceedings were interrupted by political and religious disorders. Pope Gregory XVI resumed them nearly a century later. On April 17th, 1864, Pope Pius IX approved the four miracles submitted by Cardinal Patrizi, Ponent of the Cause; and on November 20th, 1865, the solemn beatification took place in the Basilica of St. Peter at Rome. In 1864 the remains of Peter Canisius were exhumed and carried to the room of the Saint, where they were examined in the presence of the Bishop, Monsignor Marilley, by the Postulator of the Cause, two doctors and other witnesses, who were sworn in. In the following year they were transferred to the Ursuline Convent, where the nuns covered them in fine linen and laid them in a reliquary, which was encased in a marble urn and placed in the Church of St. Michel, under the Altar of the Sacred Heart Chapel—now called the Chapel of St. Peter Canisius. The last identification of the relics took place on September 10th, 1924, some months before the canonization of Peter Canisius, on 21st May, 1925.

His Holiness Pope Pius XI, on March 30th,

1925, said:[1] " The great and magnificent Peter Canisius is welcome in our age, when the sciences are taught in so many schools, when all are considered useful except the science of religion, at a time when the Press has so much prominence and exercises so much influence in social life—the Press which is the voice of the people, whom sometimes it instructs and warns and whom at other times it deceives. The life of St. Peter Canisius was occupied in the works of the apostolate, the study of sacred sciences, the propagation of Catholic truth by his doctrinal, apologetical and liturgical works, and especially by his Catechism ; and *thus he has become one of the creators of the Catholic Press and especially of the Catholic periodical*. He was one of those great souls who deny themselves and courageously endure work, fatigue and sacrifice, which is required by the apostolate for the glory of God and the welfare of souls. Lastly, in our own time, when men are divided in so many ways, it is opportune to recall the saints who have enlightened so many countries and people with the torch of their all-embracing charity. Amongst them all stands out prominently St. Peter

[1] *Saint Pierre Canisius,* par E. Morand; Fribourg, 1925, pp. 157-158. *La Libertè ;* Fribourg, Mercredi, 1 Avril, 1925.

Canisius, who was born in Holland and died in Switzerland, who was the apostle of Germany and Austria, a disciple of St. Ignatius in Rome, and a Doctor of the University of Bologna."

The Bishops of Switzerland, in their letter of May 1st, 1921, on St. Peter Canisius, say : " It is remarkable that in his large Catechism, namely, in the work which he wrote to defend the faith of tradition against current objections, he never mentions an opponent. Without mentioning contrary opinions to his own, he confines himself to establishing clearly the teaching of the church by the two-fold testimony of the Scripture and the Fathers, thinking rightly that he will obtain more valuable results by a simple exposition of the truth than by attacking error. . . . In his words it is necessary to defend the truth vigorously, but with sobriety, in order that our moderation should be manifest to all and that we should receive good testimony, if it be possible, from those who are outside the Church ; everyone requires solid proofs and a setting forth of the same with charity and humility."

By inculcating such principles, St. Peter Canisius, who was " strengthened by God in virtue and in knowledge," as the prayer of the Mass for his feast declares, was really a father in the faith to the Catholics of those countries which he evangelised.

Pope Benedict XV, in a letter to the Bishops of Switzerland, dated April 1st, 1921, says [1] : " If at a period so detrimental to religion, when the passion for novelty obscured the gold of Catholic doctrine and changed the perfect character of Christian morality, the Swiss have kept the Catholic faith, after God it must be attributed especially to the watchfulness and wisdom of this holy man." This had already been affirmed by John de Watteville, Bishop of Lausanne, in a letter sent to Pope Innocent X in 1646, as follows : " All of my diocese which has remained Catholic owes this blessing, after God, to Father Canisius." Francis Joseph Supersaxo, Bishop of Sion, wrote, in 1729, to Pope Benedict XIII : " If the new doctrines were not established either in Upper or Lower Vallais ; we owe it, after God, to Father Canisius. These countries would no longer be Catholic, if Canisius had not confirmed Fribourg and several other Cantons in the faith."

Ten years previously, in 1719, the Chief Magistrate and the Senate of Soleure made a similar declaration to Pope Clement XI, as follows : " Catholic Switzerland is indebted to Father Canisius for the preservation of the ancient faith, and for not being permitted to go astray after the example of the neighbouring countries. This man could not have rendered us a greater service." Consequently the reason is apparent why St. Peter Canisius is called the " Patriarch of Catholic Switzerland "—words that are read above his portrait, which is placed at the entrance of the choir in the Collegiate Church of St. Nicholas.

This title is also given to him by James Schueler, Dean of the Chapter, in one of his works entitled *Hercules Catholicus*, which appeared in 1651. Likewise, Claudius Anthony Duding, Bishop of Lausanne, wrote, in 1732, to Pope Clement XII as follows : " Catholic Switzerland loves Canisius as its father, honours him as its *apostle* and venerates, him as its patron." Lastly, in 1742, the Papal Nuncio did not hesitate to call St. Peter Canisius " Apostle of Switzerland."

As the Founder of the College of St. Michel, St. Peter Canisius must surely have foreseen its future development. If, in spite of the departure of the Jesuits, this college has continued to prosper, it is largely due to the influence of St. Peter Canisius. He did not plan a university for Fribourg, which at that time was a city of from five to six thousand inhabitants ; but it was rendered possible by the school for higher studies. The Bishops of Switzerland, in their letter, dated May 1st, 1921, say that the University of Fribourg has issued from the College of St. Michel as its natural complement. Deservedly this university has chosen St. Peter Canisius as its secondary patron, and every year the summer term is opened by a religious service in honour of the Apostle of Fribourg.

Dr. Charles Dändliker, a modern Swiss historian, although a non-Catholic, says of the schools at the end of the sixteenth century that [1] " the teaching of the Jesuits was at this time superior to that of Protestants."

L. Vulliemin, another Swiss Protestant writer, declares that after the arrival of St. Peter Canisius [2] "Fribourg became a centre of holy learning and devotion."

In 1585, St. Peter Canisius preached a sermon in the Church of St. Nicholas on the necessity

[1] *Geschichte der Schweiz* ; Zurich, 1885, vol. ii. p. 633.

[2] *Histoire de la Confédération Suisse* ; Lausanne, 1876, vol. ii. p. 125.

of providing better education for young girls. He said that : " It is desirable that a house should be founded in Fribourg where young girls may receive a good education. It is necessary that they should be armed against dangers of all kinds which they will meet in the world. It is necessary to come to the assistance of parents, who neither can nor will bring them up as they ought nor watch over them. Teaching these young girls Christian doctrine, teaching them to read, to write, to weave, to pray, to go to confession and to fulfil all their religious duties is an undertaking and a work of charity which merits the approval and assistance of all."

Fifty years later this project was realised by the arrival in Fribourg of the Sisters of the Visitation and the Ursuline Nuns. The Sisters of the Visitation were founded at Annecy, in 1610, by St. Francis de Sales, an admirer of St. Peter Canisius. The Ursuline Nuns are the spiritual daughters of Anne de Xainctonge, who, before the death of St. Peter Canisius, drew up a plan for the education of girls similar to his scheme. Amongst the books which she used was the Catechism of St. Peter Canisius. The Congregation founded by her in Dôle was approved in 1606 by Monsignor Doros, Bishop of Lausanne and Coadjutor to the Archbishop of Besançon.

Pope Pius XI has seen in St. Peter Canisius a precursor and a model of the apostolate by the Press. The learned Jesuit well understood the needs of his time, to which our own age bears a resemblance in many respects. He well understood the importance of writing for the spread and defence of the truth ; consequently he used all his influence to set up a printing press in Fribourg. To-day he can do nothing but bless and protect establishments of the same kind throughout the whole world, which render such valuable service to learning of all kinds. Two of these institutions in Switzerland exactly correspond to his designs ; one is called after the Apostle St. Paul, whom the Apostle of Fribourg resembles so much ; the other is named after St. Peter Canisius himself.

Such are the results of the apostolate of St. Peter Canisius. When his relics are carried in procession, they are escorted with honour by the civil and religious authorities, by the parish priests and their flocks, by the members of schools and confraternities. On May 1st, 1921, the Bishops of Switzerland wrote as follows : " We have no greater treasure than the faith. We owe a deep debt of gratitude to God, who without any merit of ours has given it to us ; for the same reason we look upon the men whom God has employed to preserve it for us as remarkable benefactors." To these benefactors, the instruments of Divine Providence, it is necessary to give signs of gratitude by paying them honour and by imitating them. In accomplishing this duty His Holiness Pope Pius XI has set St. Peter Canisius as a model before the faithful, by placing his name on the catalogue of the saints and naming him a Doctor of the Church on the 21st May, 1925.

St. Peter Canisius has been described by Father Jaccoud, Rector, in his notice of the College of St. Michel, as follows : " The portraits that we have of him, and of which several appear to have been made during his lifetime, give an impression which is in harmony with the testimony of his contemporaries and the narrative of his biographers. He was a man of middle height, somewhat thick set, with the head of an ascetic ; his countenance was oval in shape, with large, open and sparkling eyes, and a long nose, which was slightly aquiline. His mouth had a delicate expression in spite of lips which were a little hard ; he had the reserve and restrained demeanour of persons who combine great firmness and shyness ; lastly, he had an appearance of thoughtful severity, thus indicating the perfect harmony of his character. He had none of the almost irresistible affability of St. Francis de Sales ; but he was, perhaps, less austere than St. Charles Borromeo. Canisius is, without doubt, a mystic, since all the saints are more or less mystics ; but he is none the less practical. In the presence of his portrait, as in reading his books, one perceives that he has meditated deeply and prayed much ; he is an interior man and a man of God."

CHAPTER XV

ROMAN DOCUMENTS CONCERNING THE CANONIZATION OF ST. PETER CANISIUS

I. *Detailed Account of the Two Miracles submitted for the Cause of Canonization.*[1]

THE two following cures, contrary to the laws of nature, were proposed by the Postulator of the Cause, as being wrought by God through the intercession of Blessed Canisius in the Diocese of Roermond in Holland.

The first of these miracles happened to Sister Ignatia Walburga Schneller, of the Congregation of Charity of St. Francis. Her health was always weak from infancy ; in her third and fourth year she was constantly ill, being also subject to convulsions, even in childhood ; from her eleventh year to her twentieth year, almost every month, she was very much troubled with her knees. In her twenty-seventh year she joined the religious Congregation of Charity of St. Francis and, having completed the novitiate, on December

[1] *Acta Apostolicae Sedis*, 1925, vol. xvii. pp. 358-360.

12th, in the year 1896, she made her religious vows.

In the first year of her religious life she was attacked by *typhus* and her strength was nearly exhausted. In her thirtieth year she was afflicted by inflammation of the skin, which presented the appearance of measles. In the year 1904 unexpectedly she vomited blood. Two doctors endeavoured in vain to establish whether it came from the lungs or the stomach. In a short time she recovered from this sickness and regained her bodily strength. In the following year, however, the malady recurred with greater intensity, accompanied with violent pains in the stomach, and was of more frequent occurrence. Eventually in the year 1910 medical aid was sought. The doctor, thinking that Sister Ignatia was suffering from strangulated hernia, carried out a surgical operation, from which, contrary to expectation, it appeared that her illness was consumption of the bowels. Consequently, Dr. Rembauts, who had performed the surgical operation, considered that the part affected with tuberculosis should be removed.

After this surgical operation Sister Ignatia was somewhat better for some years; but she was by no means restored to perfect health. Although she was accustomed to take the greatest precautions and to eat light food, in the year 1915 she began again to be afflicted with frequent vomiting and violent pains in the stomach, sometimes being scarcely able and sometimes being unable to walk upright. In the beginning of the year 1921 these infirmities were increased to such a degree that Sister Ignatia was unable to retain even liquid nourishment, and, confined to her bed, she was compelled to lie on her back on account of pains in her chest and back. Dr. Kettler, who diligently examined her, decided that she had rapid consumption of the bowels and, therefore, a fresh surgical operation was necessary. Specialists who were engaged, Drs. Henry Pomponi, Albert Ciotola and Nicholas Gentile declared that Sister Ignatia was suffering from chronic stoppage of the bowels brought on by tubercular affection.

Since all human remedies were of no avail, and death seemed to approach, Sister Mary Cornelia Casimir, the Mother-General, resolved to implore the assistance of God by means of the patronage of Blessed Peter Canisius. Having procured a relic of him from the Fathers of the Society of Jesus, a novena was begun in the convent, Masses being said daily and fervent prayers offered for this end. And it was not in vain. When the relic of Blessed Canisius was applied to the Sister who was ill, instantly she felt better, and, quicker than one would have supposed, she was restored to perfect health, every trace of the very serious illness being removed.

The other miracle happened in the College of St. Ignatius which the Jesuits have at Valkenberg, a town of the Netherlands in the Diocese of Roermond. Brother Peter Schmitz, a scholastic of the same Society, who was twenty-four years old, had hardly recovered from influenza when, a few days later, on January 12th, in the year 1922, he was taken ill with inflammation of the throat with an abscess. A doctor having been summoned the abscess was lanced, and the patient experienced some relief, the fever seeming to disappear; but, contrary to expectation, he became worse, the fever returned with greater inflammation, accompanied by sharp pains in the limbs and back, which spread to his arms, hands, feet and sides. His heart became weak and his breathing difficult. He disliked food and could not bear the light, while his pulse was weak, irregular and very rapid. Doctors Hapig and Kettler, who were in attendance, having considered these features of his sickness, after a consultation, were convinced that it was a case of septic poisoning.

This verdict of fatal septic poisoning, given by the two doctors who had undertaken his cure, was clearly confirmed afterwards by the specialists summoned, namely, Doctors Francis Xavier Armellini, Francis Pagano and Boleslaus Madeyski. On account of the character and seriousness of this sickness, Dr. Kettler, thinking that no hope of recovery remained, proposed a serum injection, which, having been administered and repeated, lacked the desired effect. As the sick man appeared to be dying, he was fortified with the Last Sacraments. All human aid having failed, the sick man and his companions with confidence invoked the intercession of Blessed Peter Canisius by beginning a novena. The Rector of the college offered a relic of Blessed Peter (viz., a part of one of his fingers) to the sick man, who afterwards always carried it on his breast. When the novena was ended, the fever began to increase again, and the doctors declared his case hopeless.

Consequently a second novena was made, and the Sacrifice of the Mass was offered daily. The sick man frequently during the day kissed the relic which was offered to him and applied it to the weak parts of his body and especially his heart. He prayed daily for the canonization of Blessed Peter Canisius, adding the recitation of three *Hail Marys*. Now God did not disappoint the sick man and his religious associates; for by the intercession of Blessed Canisius it happened that he who, on February 7th, appeared to be at the point of death, on the following day, in the morning, contrary to expectation, was out of danger and straightway was restored to quite perfect health.—"Decretal Letter of Pope Pius XI concerning the canonization of St. Peter Canisius."

II. *Decree of the Sacred Congregation of Rites approving the Miracles for the Canonization of Blessed Peter Canisius.*[1]

Here two divisions are to be observed: Firstly, the facts are examined; secondly, the rules of canon law are applied to them. Following this procedure, the advocates of

[1] *Acta Apostolicae Sedis*, 1925, vol. xvii. pp. 156-158.

the Sacred Congregation considered the first
miracle, namely, the cure of Sister Ignatia
Walburga Schneller. From the records of
this case, which are to be found in the archives,
and from the testimony given by the best
informed eye-witnesses under oath, the advocates ascertained and proved the following
facts, namely, that Sister Ignatia, who had
suffered from stoppage of the bowels, was in
the greatest peril of her life. Nevertheless,
the same Sister Ignatia, who, until then
remained in a dying condition, had hardly
touched the relic of Blessed Peter Canisius
than, contrary to what was generally supposed,
the doctor in attendance leading the way in
his avowal,—she, I will not say did not die
but lived and was cured. She was restored
to her former health and all were astonished
and amazed, since a little while previously
there had been no discharge from her
stomach worthy of note nor had there been
a surgical operation.

Now these facts have to be considered from
the point of view of canon law. In technical
questions of this kind it is necessary to hear
the testimony of men skilled in their art,
amongst whom must be reckoned the doctor
who attended Sister Ignatia. He knew well

that the stoppage of the bowels, which had so cruelly troubled Sister Ignatia, was not the disease but was to be considered and was in reality the symptom of a disease. Therefore he proceeded to the cause of the disease, whence the symptom just mentioned was derived, and he saw that it consisted in tubercular affection. Thus, having recognised and established the nature of the disease, the doctor in attendance declared and testified more than once that only in a surgical operation was there hope of recovery and a remedy for avoiding certain death. Nor was his opinion false, which was admitted and plainly declared by three specialists, appointed to deliver judgment, whose authority is supreme in all tribunals.

This is deservedly so, seeing that they are summoned in that capacity and are bound by the sanctity of an oath. Consequently, Benedict XIV, writing about them, says that their judgment in this Sacred Congregation *is reckoned of more value than that of others who . . . have given aid in the cure of the sick person ;* and to whom *it pertains especially to weigh carefully the reasons brought forward by others, to examine carefully their points, and to put in the balance the causes and symptoms of the disease related by the doctors of the sick person* (Lib. IV. p. 1. c. 8, num. 4, 5).

Thus if anyone considers the two parts of this question (the first of which is entirely based on fact, and the second which concerns canon law, the science of medicine and surgery), and carefully compares them in relation to each other, a clear proof of the miracle will be inevitably ascertained, as was established by the three specialists who were employed in that capacity by the Sacred Congregation. Their united and unanimous verdict was that the cure of Sister Ignatia could be only attributed to a miracle.

Likewise reference is to be made to the second cure or miracle, the subject of which was Brother Peter Schmitz of the Society of Jesus. In order to fulfil the conditions laid down in canon law and to establish the truth of the facts, the three following points were submitted to the Patron of the Cause for proof : firstly, that it was really a case of septic poisoning ; secondly, that no influence or efficacy was to be assigned to the serum injection ; thirdly, that a sudden and perfect cure took place. These three things were proved to the Patron, as is made known by

13

the further examination and reading found in the Epitome of the Cause. Being thus convinced, the Patron hastened to bring forward valid and suitable proofs. The written approbation of the three experts summoned to give judgment is of the greatest value, and especially the testimony given by the third expert, who was uncommonly skilled in discerning and curing disease and excelled in practical knowledge. Therefore the usual title of specialist, derived from the particular knowledge for which his services were sought, suitably designates him.

The rules of canon law were applied at the beginning, during the course and at the conclusion of the examination of the Cause, with the results described as follows : After the preliminary and preparatory sessions had been held, a general assembly was convened on the 24th day of March, in the presence of Our Holy Father Pope Pius XI. At this meeting Cardinal Vico, the Ponent of the Cause, submitted the following question for solution :—

" Is there satisfactory evidence that, since the permission of the Holy See to venerate Blessed Peter Canisius, miracles have been worked

*in the case in point and to the effect in
question ? "*

The Cardinals and Consultors gave their
votes in the affirmative, and His Holiness
accepted their verdict; but, as is customary,
he reserved judgment that time might be
given for repeated prayers to seek the fulness
of light from heaven. When he had decided
to make known his judgment, he chose
Passion Sunday. After Holy Mass he summoned to the Vatican the Most Rev. Cardinal
Vico, Bishop of Porto and Santa Rufina,
Prefect of the Sacred Congregation of Rites
and Ponent of the Cause, as also Rev. Father
Angelus Mariani, Promoter of the Faith, and
the undersigned Secretary. There, in our
presence, the Pope solemnly declared : *It is
evident that the two cures submitted are real
and true miracles ; the first being the immediate
and perfect cure of stoppage of the bowels
brought on by tubercular affection in the case
of Sister Ignatia Walburga Schneller ; the
second being the immediate and perfect cure of
the fatal disease of septic poisoning in the case
of Brother Peter Schmitz, of the Society of Jesus.*

The Pope also gave command that this
Decree should be published and preserved in
the archives of the Sacred Congregation of

Rites the fourth day before the calends of April (the 29th March), 1925.

      ✠ A. CARDINAL VICO, *Bishop of Porto and Santa Rufina, Prefect of the Sacred Congregation of Rites.*

      ALEXANDER VERDE, *Secretary of the S.C.R.*

L. ✠ S.

III. *Decree of the Sacred Congregation of Rites concerning the Solemn Canonization of Blessed Peter Canisius.*[1]

The quality and extent of the merits by which the Cause of the Canonization of Blessed Peter Canisius is distinguished and enriched are declared and plainly indicated by his whole life and achievements. But to relate in detail and to follow faithfully what Blessed Peter Canisius did and accomplished throughout the course of his life, which spanned seventy-seven years, would certainly be a very long task, although it would be very pleasant to hear and would greatly benefit all Christendom. Nevertheless, it is not difficult for a prudent man and for one

[1] *Acta Apostolicae Sedis*, 1925, vol. xvii, pp. 197-199.

who has an accurate and true judgment of events briefly to relate the very abundant and no less remarkable benefits resulting from his deeds, as well as to view and to weigh them in one comprehensive glance. After diligent examination, he can only straightway be led to the conclusion and avowal that from these two things, as from their original and primary source, and as from their very foundation, all without exception is derived, namely, from his well-known sanctity, in which he excelled, and from his remarkable and extraordinary erudition, for which he became renowned.

Clearly the Almighty and Merciful God raised him up in order that, fortified as it were with a two-edged sword, he might wholly apply himself to reform the corrupt morals of the people and to rebuke and refute heresy which was spread far and wide. God Himself presaged what was to be the special mission or vocation of Blessed Peter Canisius, as may be inferred from the circumstances attending his birth. At the beginning of the first of the three historic lessons, which have been approved by the Sacred Congregation of Rites for his feast, the following words are read : *Peter Canisius was born at Nymwegen in Gueldre in the very year in which Luther, in Germany, after an open revolt, withdrew from the church, and Ignatius Loyola, in Spain, having given up a worldly military service, devoted himself to fighting the battles of the Lord. Thus God betokened the adversaries, whom he was to have hereafter, and his leader in holy warfare.* Indeed, under the guidance and rule laid down by the teaching of his spiritual father, Ignatius Loyola, the advance and progress made by Peter Canisius, the constancy and fidelity with which he adhered to his mission or vocation, and how fully and abundantly he accomplished it, have been proved in a wonderful manner by the events which happened in Peter's early years in the various stages of his life and after his death in the constant yet varied succession of the centuries.

On this occasion it is worth while to select two achievements, as previously related in the Apostolic Decree, by means of which the Supreme Pontiff of sacred memory, Pope Pius IX, in 1864, conferred upon Peter Canisius the honours of the Blessed. He was in his twenty-sixth year when Cardinal Otto Truchsess, Bishop of Augsburg, knowing well his knowledge and virtue, sent him to the Council of Trent with the title and in the capacity of theologian. In a full assembly of the Fathers of the Catholic Church, his learning in the discussions, the timeliness of his counsel in explaining questions, his promptitude in reply, his energy and firmness in giving his opinion, were proved to all. He was zealous in the defence of Catholic truth and took the greatest pains in the true and sound education of youth. He strove with perseverance in his endeavour that again undefiled doctrine and scholastic theology should be publicly taught, summoning to teach masters tried in the faith. When he perceived that poison was spread among the people by Protestants, through books abounding in errors, in order to provide a timely remedy for so great an evil, he himself wrote a *Manual of Christian Doctrine*, which was received with unanimous applause by bishops and theologians and was spread everywhere for the good of souls.

He was appointed by St. Ignatius to be the first Provincial of the German Province, and he erected colleges everywhere for the education of youth. He used every endeavour that the *German College* should be

permanently established in Rome to receive
young men of that nation who, under the
auspices of the Roman Pontiffs, having been
trained in good morals and educated in true
doctrine, would return to their country as
the soldiers of Christ, bravely to conquer
widespread heresy.

Here we must stop. The limits assigned
to this Apostolic Decree would indeed not
allow us to proceed further. Therefore, in
order to return to the starting point of this
theme, anyone who may be only a little
versed in the history of the church and of
nations cannot fail to observe the sanctity
for which Blessed Peter Canisius was distinguished, the erudition for which he was
eminent, and how, in his person, both were
joined in the closest harmony. But to
recognise and proclaim these things is equi-
valent to recognising and proclaiming the
merits by which this most excellent cause
of Blessed Peter Canisius, being powerfully
and abundantly drawn up and prepared,
reaches the highest dignity of canonization,
since by its action and vote, as was just,
this Sacred Congregation especially recognised and approved it in the General Assembly
which was held on the 24th day of this

month of March, in the presence of His Holiness Pope Pius XI.

For, as at a more recent time, owing to particular circumstances intervening, the process was conducted in the Cause of Canonization of Rita a Cassia, who was Blessed at that time, so in the same General Assembly the following questions were submitted for solution : "*Is there satisfactory evidence that, since the permission of the Holy See to venerate Blessed Peter Canisius, miracles have been worked in the case in point and to the effect in question?*" and "*On the supposition that approval has been given to the miracles, may one with all security proceed to his solemn canonization?*" When the second question was likewise submitted by Cardinal Vico, the Ponent of the Cause, the Cardinals and Consultors who were present gave their votes in the affirmative. His Holiness accepted their verdict, and in a matter of such importance he willed that all should be asked to pray to obtain for himself the heavenly light and help of the Holy Spirit.

On Passion Sunday, after Holy Mass, the Pope gave command that the Most Rev. Cardinal Vico, Bishop of Porto and Santa Rufina, Prefect of the Sacred Congregation of Rites and Ponent of the Cause, and also Rev. Father Angelus Mariani, Promoter of the Faith, and the undersigned Secretary, should be summoned to the Vatican. There, in our presence, the Pope solemnly declared : "*One may with all security proceed to the solemn canonization of Blessed Peter Canisius.*"

The Pope gave command that this Decree should be published and preserved in the archives of the Sacred Congregation of Rites, also that an Apostolic Decree under the seal should be issued concerning the solemnities of the canonization, to be held in St. Peter's on a day to be fixed by His Holiness, the fourth day before the calends of April (29th March), 1925.

✠ A. CARDINAL VICO, *Bishop of Porto and Santa Rufina, Prefect of the Sacred Congregation of Rites.*

ALEXANDER VERDE,
Secretary of the S.C.R.

L. ✠ S.

IV. *Homily of Pope Pius XI on the occasion of the Canonization of St. Peter Canisius, Feast of the Ascension, May 21st, 1925[1].*

Venerable Brethren and Beloved Sons,

"Christ the Lord, being mindful of His promise, not only never fails Holy Church in seasonable aid, but also in all troubled times has been wont to raise up men of the greatest worth in holiness, *mighty in work and in word* (see Luke xxiv. 19), to defend bravely His kingdom on earth and to spread it far and wide. Thus especially, in Christendom's hour of need, Peter Canisius, a most renowned defender and an apostle of the faith, emerged, when indeed what is truly so-called a new assistance was given by God through Ignatius Loyola to the Church Militant.

"This excellent member of the newly formed Society of Jesus benefited, not by one title only, the Spouse of Jesus Christ in her trial. He benefited her indeed by the example of all the virtues, in which, from childhood to extreme old age, he made such wonderful progress that he excited the greatest admiration of his contemporaries.

[1] *Acta Apostolicae Sedis*, 1925, vol. xvii. pp. 215-218.

He benefited her also by his knowledge of literature and by his most excellent teaching of divine truth, which he supported by constantly reading Holy Scripture and the works of the Fathers.

" Since he combined the light of the wisdom of the schools with a thorough knowledge of positive theology, as it is called, there is no reason for surprise that he went into the fray as a thoroughly equipped soldier to attack the monstrous errors of heretics. In a word, he benefited her by the labours which he undertook and endured for about fifty years, having refused any respite ; for continually, during this time, as he strove to restore the discipline of the clergy and the morality of the people—also inspiring courage in those placed in authority over Christian peoples to exercise vigilance and diligence—so he never ceased to oppose heresy and the vices which prepare the way to heresy.

" Accordingly this newly-canonized saint, who—being born in Gueldre in the very year in which Ignatius of Spain reformed himself and began to live a more perfect life, and the separation of some of the provinces of Germany from the Roman Church began to

be effected—possessed the honest and most
steadfast character of the Dutch people, by
the command of his spiritual father, Ignatius,
and his own Superiors, as well as the Sovereign
Pontiff, was appointed to that mission to
which, in prayer at the tomb of St. Peter in
this magnificent temple, he had understood
that he was called by God as another
Boniface. Since he knew well that the grace
of the Holy Spirit does not observe slow
endeavours—leaving the secluded and dearly
beloved training school of his religious house,
like a combatant appearing in public—without
any delay he hastened to take charge of the
Province assigned to him.

" Very many difficulties, perils of life,
snares of enemies, indignities and insults,
inconveniences of travelling, combined with
fasting and cares, did not deter the toiler, of
spirited resolution, from his undertaking ;
for he considered that the Apostles of Christ
' went from the presence of the council
rejoicing that they were accounted worthy
to suffer reproach for the name of Christ '
(Acts v. 41), and ' all that will live godly in
Christ Jesus shall suffer persecution ' (2 Tim.
iii. 12). Therefore he confirmed his fellow
Catholics in the faith, and with perseverance

helped the return of heretics to the Church,
whether he taught pupils entrusted to him,
or preached in churches. As often as there
was a question of faith or morals, he had
no peer in debates with reformers, either in
Athenaeums, or in public assemblies, or in
the market place.

" The fact that opponents, in jest, dubbed
him ' The Dog ' certainly redounds to his
praise and honour ; for, as a faithful dog,
he dispersed all who attacked the flock
of the Lord, not only by raising his voice
but also by offering resistance. Where it
was not possible for him to be present and
to speak, even there his writings penetrated.
Especially wonderful is his Catechism, which,
translated into nearly all languages and spread
throughout the world, especially in those
countries in which the greatest danger of
heresy was imminent, gave rise to joy in the
victory of true Catholic doctrine. No less
did Canisius contribute to the defence of
Catholic doctrine by his letters, now col-
lected in many volumes, and by his writings
directed against the Centuriators, which,
although they were interrupted for very
urgent reasons by the command of superiors,
were yet an inducement to Cardinal Baronius,

of immortal memory, to fill his place by composing his *Annales*.

" Indeed the very conspicuous abundance and impressiveness of the teaching of the second Apostle of Germany, after Boniface, which our predecessor Leo XIII, in his encyclical, twenty-seven years ago (August 1st, 1897), solemnised with praise which seemed hardly to be suitable for one to whom the title of Doctor had not yet been assigned, has quite induced us, with one and the same decision, to enrol Canisius among the saints of Heaven and the doctors of the Church, as we have done a little while before, and as we are soon about to proclaim by a Decretal Letter. We were urged to form this resolution by letters of supplication, as they are termed, which have been given to us not long previously, by several bishops, theological faculties and universities.

" Since, moreover, the activity and apostolate of this newly-canonized saint and doctor extended to very many nations, namely, to Alsace and Switzerland, Bohemia and Poland, Austria, Hungary and Italy, where he made wonderful provision for the education of youth and the foundation of seminaries and colleges, does not God Himself, on this particular occasion, seem to present him to all nations for veneration and imitation as a token of unity and peace ? Oh, that it may be the good fortune of us all who honour to-day the triumphal return of Our Redeemer to the Father, that, having followed the footsteps of St. Peter Canisius, and relying on his patronage, we, at length, may have our lot for everlasting ages with Christ, to Whom be praise, honour and glory for ever and ever. Amen."

INDEX

[The figures refer to pages of the Book.]

Made and Printed in Ireland by Browne and Nolan Limited